Sweet Potatoes Cooking School

Presents

Wicked Good Food

By

Matt Williams

iUniverse, Inc.
New York Bloomington

Sweet Potatoes Cooking School Presents Wicked Good Food

iUniverse Star
an iUniverse, Inc. imprint

iUniverse books may be ordered through booksellers or by contacting:

iUniverse
1663 Liberty Drive
Bloomington, IN 47403
www.iuniverse.com
1-800-Authors (1-800-288-4677)

ISBN: 978-1-936236-26-8 (sc)
ISBN: 978-1-936236-27-5 (ebook)

Library of Congress Control Number: 2010912270

Printed in the United States of America

iUniverse rev. date: 10/18/2010

*To everyone who has ever cooked something
inedible yet kept on cooking.*

Play with Your Food!

Contents

Preface

When I was a kid, I loved macaroni and cheese and cream of tomato soup. Now that I'm an adult and an accomplished chef, I love macaroni and cheese and cream of tomato soup. Although some of it surely is, great food doesn't need to be complex or time-consuming. Albert Einstein said, "Make everything as simple as possible, but not simpler." Although I don't think I ever said these words aloud, this has always been my motto for cooking.

I first began professionally cooking at age sixteen and haven't looked back since. Since earning associate's, bachelor's, and graduate degrees from Johnson and Wales University, I've been fortunate to work in and travel to just about every corner of the United States, but I've always seemed to make my way back to the ocean and Massachusetts. The people I've met through these travels, what I learned from them, how they learned from me, and all the things I've eaten have helped define me as a chef and an educator. Even in my role as the culinary arts team leader at Blackstone Valley Tech and as the one people come to when looking for food answers, I've stayed as excited as ever to ask my own questions and learn by playing with my food.

The biggest thrill I get from cooking is seeing people's reactions as they enjoy my food. I love the challenge of learning someone's likes and dislikes and playing with a recipe to make it perfect for them. While taking other people's tastes into account, a dish must please me before I present it to someone else. These are the same goals I have when teaching throughout central Massachusetts through my Sweet Potatoes Cooking School. Here I can share my knowledge and experience with students in the privacy of their own kitchens and teach them exactly what they want to know.

Apparently I've gotten pretty good at doing this because I'm often asked how I made something or whether I can send someone a recipe. I cannot think of anything I enjoy talking about more than food, but handwriting a recipe every time someone asks for one has gotten old.

That was my inspiration for writing this book. It began as a collection of recipes to share with family, friends, students, and people who wanted to talk about food. As time passed, the collection grew and so did my memories about particular dishes, including the first time I tasted them or how I created them. Growing up in New England, people, especially my grandfather, would refer to things as wicked good whenever they were really impressed. Wicked good is how I would describe the recipes in this book, so I decided it was a fitting name for the whole book.

I'm excited to be able to share all of this with you and your family, friends, and maybe even students. Throughout the book you'll find a number of hints and tips to help you along the way, as well as a glossary of over one hundred terms, identified by boldface in the text. The underlying idea is that anyone—from a complete novice to a seasoned cook—will be able to find something useful or interesting on every page. I consider every recipe in this book, including macaroni and cheese and cream of tomato soup, to be Wicked Good Food.

I hope you do too.

Acknowledgments

To God, without whom nothing in this book, or any other book, would be possible.

To my parents, who have given every possible advantage they could to my brother and me and always encouraged me to play with my food.

To my beautiful wife, Jane, who allowed me to spend countless hours on the computer working on "the book."

To all the dishwashers, students, cooks, chefs, and foodies who have been kind enough to teach me and talk food with me.

To Mr. B, who taught me more about teaching while sitting at his desk than all my professors combined.

To all my family and friends, for their constant love and support.

To those who helped me proofread and edit, test recipes, and develop the ideas for *Wicked Good Food*:
Rob Cummings
Pastors Allen and Sara Ewing-Merrill
Steve and Tina Zicari
Corey Bunnewith
Pastor Doug Robinson Johnson
Amanda Pape
Sandy Mckeown
Jill Pfendner
Dave Rosati
Dean Wood

Sterling Ryan Doster
Scott Kogos
Carolin Collins
Bo and Naomi Phaneuf
Fred and Kate Pape
Joe and Joyce Siano
Pastors Dan Crede and Gay King Crede
Leah Okimoto
Chris and Lindsey Cusson
Nate and Becky Hequembourg
Beth Fenstermacher
Bill and Kim Powazinik
Josh Bridgewater
Rebecca Swasey
Jim Provencher—designer of the Sweet Potato guy

And to anyone I forgot—
thank you.

Introduction

How to Cook

Okay, well, you can't really learn to cook from reading a book, but I'm going to try and provide you with some basics to help you, through practice, become a better cook. Even without practice, the vast majority of the recipes and tips in this book are suitable for very novice cooks who want to venture from their comfort zones a bit.

The secret of every great cook is an understanding of how ingredients work together and a knowledge of **cooking methods**. That's it. It's not dependent on the right knife, the proper size pan, or the correct type of mixer. You can put an indifferent or inexperienced cook in the best-equipped kitchen on the planet, and while it may stoke his or her ego, it will not improve the food the person cooks. Put someone with a passion for and a basic understanding of cooking in a tiny kitchen, without great knives or pans or mixers, and watch and smell and, if you're lucky, taste what he or she can do.

Developing an understanding of how ingredients work together is more difficult than learning cooking methods, but it is also more fun. That's mostly because you get to eat stuff. Don't be afraid to walk through your local market and buy something you've never seen before or try and re-create a dish you had at that restaurant the other night. Go home and play!

The best advice I have for learning ingredients is to think about what you're doing and why. Keep a notebook in your kitchen, and jot down notes on all the successes—and maybe more importantly—the failures you have in the kitchen. Never be afraid to ask questions of knowledgeable people, whether they be your mother or the farmer at your closest farmers' market. While cooking you should constantly taste, then think about what you just tasted. Then taste it again. You'll be amazed at what you can taste when you really think about it.

Try having a tasting in your own kitchen where you compare salts, peppers, vinegars, or oils. All varieties of these ingredients have different characteristics, and each will have an effect on the final flavor and sometimes texture of a recipe. Almost all of the recipes in this book call for **kosher salt** and freshly ground black pepper. I think these have the best flavor, but you don't need to trust me. Make your own comparisons, and use what you prefer.

Don't feel the need to buy only brand-name ingredients. Many store-branded items are just as good as and sometimes better than big brand names. Find one you like, and stick with it.

When it comes to shopping for your food, try to use fresh, local ingredients as often as possible. They support the local agriculture, they typically have less pesticides or chemicals used to promote a longer shelf life, they are fresher, and most importantly, they taste better. That's not to mention the connection formed when you can talk to the person who actually took the time and care to grow what you're about to eat or see the land it was grown on. Go and tour local farms, wineries, orchards, breweries, bakeries, and factories that make your food. All of these experiences will help you understand where our food comes from and what is involved in producing it. This knowledge will make you a better cook. Next time you drive past a farmers' market or local farm stand, stop by and see what's fresh. Take the challenge to plan your meal around that!

Without great ingredients, one cannot make great food; however, even with great ingredients, it's quite easy to make terrible food. This is where knowledge of cooking methods is handy. Most of us have used all of these methods before but may not have known that there was a name for them and some science behind why we use them. There are only about a dozen different methods, but each will produce a different result when used on the same piece of food.

Cooking methods are divided into three categories: dry, moist, and combination. Dry methods are cooked in a dry environment and do not have any moisture added to them. Moist methods use some sort of liquid as a cooking medium. The cooking liquid can be water, but the more flavor the liquid has, the more flavor the final product will have. Combination methods are a two-step process where cooking first involves a dry method and then is finished with a moist method, typically using a flavored liquid.

Grilling and **broiling**, which are both dry methods, are great for many vegetables and tender meats. Meats such as chicken, pork loin, beef tenderloin, and firm-fleshed fish are great cooked with these methods because they don't need any extra tenderizing and are firm enough to stay in one piece on the grill.

When translated from the French, to **sauté** literally means "to jump." Sautéing begins with a very hot pan to which a small amount of fat is quickly added, followed by food. The food is then moved around the pan, either by flipping the pan or stirring, so that all surfaces of the food come in contact with the hot pan. Sautéing is great for small pieces of meat and vegetables that can be cooked quickly and can also add flavor and color. Often once items are **seared,** a liquid is added to **deglaze** the pan of any remaining pieces of food. The resulting flavorful liquid is used to build a sauce. Sautéing is very similar to **stir-frying**, but stir-frying is typically done in a very hot **wok** and the food is stirred and not necessarily flipped.

Baking and **roasting** are other dry cooking methods that are good for tender meats, especially ones that are too large or delicate for a grill or broiler. Roasting is also good for meats that are not tender and require a long, slow cooking process, such as pork butt for pulled pork. Long, slow cooking helps tenderize the meat by breaking down some of its fibers. Baking is also the method we use for baked goods such as cookies and breads. Even, dry heat provides the perfect place for **leaveners** to work. Baking and roasting can be done in a standard oven or in a **convection** oven, which is a regular oven with a fan inside. The fan keeps the oven evenly hot and constantly surrounds items being cooked with air that is hot and has not been cooled down by the food. This is still baking or roasting, but the cooking time is reduced by up to a third.

Believe it or not, **deep-frying** and **shallow frying** are dry cooking methods. Even though the oil you fry with is liquid, the method is not considered a moist cooking medium because properly fried foods should have very little contact with the hot oil. When the food is put into the oil, the moisture in the food turns to steam and forces its way out, making the fryer bubble. During this time, the pressure of the steam escaping prevents the oil from going into the food. Fried foods get greasy and taste like oil if they're left in the fryer so long that there's not enough steam to keep the oil out.

When frying at home, you need to take a number of precautions, especially if you don't have a fryer and are using a pot on the stove. First and most importantly, do not walk away from the kitchen while you have a fry pot going. Try to use a **heavy gauge** pot that will help distribute the heat evenly. Heavy gauge means that the metal, especially on the bottom of the pot, is thicker than normal. Use enough oil to completely submerge whatever you're frying, plus a couple inches extra. Use a pot with a height twice the depth of your oil to help prevent splattering or boiling over when you add food.

Most fried foods are cooked at a temperature of between 350 and 375 degrees. A good-quality candy or deep-frying thermometer is needed to measure the temperature and keep it consistent. Do not fry without knowing the temperature of your oil. If the oil is extremely overheated, it will begin to smoke and can eventually burst into flames. Because the oil is extremely hot, carefully lower food into it so that the oil doesn't splash back at you. Remove cooked items with a basket or slotted spoon. Put the food on a metal rack placed inside of a sheet pan to allow excess oil to drain.

Try to fry in small batches so that you don't overcrowd your oil and cause the oil temperature to drop. If the oil is not at a high enough temperature, the food will take longer to cook and will also become greasy. If you have lots of batches to fry, keep previously fried items warm and crispy by placing them in a pan in a 200-degree oven.

A number of different oils are good for frying, and a bunch are not very good. Most of the oils that don't work well cannot handle the high heat of frying, are so flavorful that they would overpower the flavor of the food you're frying, or are just too expensive to warrant using for frying. When I fry at home, I use a quality vegetable oil that I buy by the gallon. After you finish frying, allow the oil to cool completely, strain through a fine strainer, funnel back into the bottle, and seal tightly until the next time you fry. Never try to put hot oil back in the bottle, as it will melt, make a mess, and probably burn you in the process.

Boiling, simmering, and **poaching** are all moist methods where food is placed directly into hot liquid. The temperature of the water and the amount of **convection movement** (bubbling) determines which of these methods you're using. Boiling has a rapid convection movement that makes it suitable for foods that are not fragile and need to be kept moving, such as pasta. Simmering liquid does not move as violently as boiling and is great for most foods, especially vegetables. Poaching is used for the most tender and fragile products, such as eggs. It involves very little movement and will not damage foods as much as boiling would.

Steaming is another moist method, even though the food is never placed into the hot liquid. With steaming, food is suspended, oftentimes in a basket, above a hot liquid in a covered vessel. Having a cover on the pot increases the pressure inside and prevents steam from escaping. This allows the temperature of the steam to rise and the food to cook faster. Steaming is favored for many vegetables and delicate fish because it is gentle and also because it results in little loss of nutrients and requires no added fat.

There are two combination methods. They are essentially the same process, but **stewing** uses smaller pieces of meat, such as stew beef, and **braising** is for a large piece of meat, such as a pot roast. These methods are typically reserved for meat that requires a long, moist cooking process for tenderness. In the initial dry step, the meat is seared in a hot pan or hot oven to develop deeper and more complex flavor and color. A liquid is then added to cover the meat, and it is cooked, either in the oven or on the stovetop, until the meat is tender.

However simple it may seem, being familiar with even just a few of these methods and knowing about a couple of ingredients is all the "education" one needs to become a better cook. The rest is just playing with your food and remembering what worked, what didn't, and why. Whenever you can, ask yourself why a recipe, a friend, or a cooking show tells you do to something in a particular way or at a certain time. If you cannot figure out the answer, ask questions. That is the best way to learn.

Cooking is an art open to seemingly endless possibilities. However, it is all based on a foundation of science and is influenced by all the generations that came before. Where and how they lived, what they could grow or forage or hunt for, and the technology and time in which they did all these things determined the cuisine of all parts of the world at all times.

We live in an exciting time in which we can find ingredients and recipes from across the entire world. All these raw ingredients and information can be overwhelming to a beginning cook. Start with things you like, and understand why as well as how they are made. The more you play with your food and think about what you've done, the easier it is for you to stop following recipes as if they are law and add more of your own twists to make recipes more your own. Be careful, though. As you develop your own repertoire of signature dishes, more people are going to ask for them. You may find yourself dedicating two years of your life to writing your own cookbook.

Stuff You Should Have

All a basic kitchen needs is a cutting board, a good knife, something that will get hot, and some pans. Almost everything else is bonus. I'm not a big fan of kitchen gadgets, but there are a number of tools that are useful. The following items are used in this book, and in my kitchen, to make life easier. They aren't required items for cooking, but once you use them, you may find yourself asking what you ever did before you had them.

<u>Knives</u>

Besides your hands, which should be used for everything you possibly can, your knives are the most important tools in the kitchen. There are hundreds of types of knives out there, but I almost always use one of four types.

A French, or chef's, knife is an all-purpose knife used for chopping and slicing meats and vegetables. These knives can be very short or very long. I prefer an eight-inch blade for most of my cooking. A paring knife is a short knife used for peeling, removing cores, and other fine work. A boning knife has a relatively narrow blade that comes to a sharp point. It is used for removing bones, fat, and other material from meat prior to cooking. A serrated knife is typically long with a number of scalloped edges on the blade. It is great for cutting bread without crushing it, as well as cutting vegetables with skins, such as tomatoes.

When choosing knives, don't let price be a deciding factor. I have one chef knife I love that cost me about $150 and another that I use quite often that cost me four dollars at a discount store. Both knives have a lot in common. Most importantly, they feel good in my hand. They are well balanced, and my hand doesn't get tired from using them. Make sure there's enough room for your fingers to grip the handle without having them touch your cutting board while cutting. This area of the blade from the bottom of the handle to the end of the blade is called the **heel**.

How a knife is made is also important. You want a knife made of a high-carbon stainless steel. (While not technically stainless, that's what they're called.) This metal is good because it has enough carbon in it to make the blade soft enough to sharpen but enough steel in it to hold an edge and prevent the blade from becoming stained. You also want a knife with a full **tang**—the part of the blade that extends to the handle. A tang that goes all the way through the handle results in a stronger knife that will last longer.

Keeping your knives sharp is just as important as selecting the knife that is right for you. A knife comes from the factory with a very sharp edge, but it won't seem so sharp for long. As a knife is used, the edge of the blade tends to get bent or dinged a bit. Using a **steel** to **hone** your knife will quickly and easily straighten the edge of the blade. I recommend running your knife over a steel before each use. This is done by sliding the entire edge of the knife blade, from heel to tip, across the entire length of the steel. Try to keep your knife at a 45 degree angle

Eventually using a steel will not be enough, and your knife will need to be sharpened. There are some mechanical knife sharpeners that are good for occasionally used knives, but they can remove a lot of metal. If you use your knife frequently and want it to last a number of years, it is worth getting it professionally sharpened or learning how to sharpen using a stone. Sharpening actually shapes or creates an edge on your knife, whereas using a steel to hone the knife only straightens the edge that is already there.

Pots and pans

The pots and pans you need depend a lot on what you plan to cook. I recommend having one smaller, six-to-eight-inch sauté pan and one larger, ten-to-twelve-inch sauté pan. A sauté pan is a shallow pan with one long handle and curved sides that aid in tossing food. A nonstick coating is great on these; however, be careful not to overheat them when empty because they can release harmful chemicals at high temperatures.

I also recommend a medium-sized sauce pan, about two and a half quarts, and a large sauce pan that's about four quarts. A sauce pan is a smaller pan with one handle and tall sides. It's used for most moist cooking methods, as well as for making soups and sauces.

In addition, I like to have a larger pot with a **heavy gauge** metal. This helps keep food from burning and ensures a more even distribution of heat. I recommend a size of ten quarts or so. A pot of this size is great for **searing** things for stews, cooking pasta, and cooking foods for long periods of time.

Next on the shopping list are a couple of sheet pans or cookie sheets. Buy them as large as your oven will hold as they are invaluable for making the most of your oven space. You can either cook directly on them or place them below a baking dish to help keep your oven clean. I prefer pans with sides instead of flat sheets, as these have more uses.

Baking dishes come in a number of shapes and sizes and materials. There are some small benefits of one over another, but it all boils down to personal preference. Have at least one large, shallow dish and one smaller but deeper dish.

As you cook more, you may decide that you need different types and sizes of pans, but this is a good start.

Cast-iron skillet

A cast-iron skillet that is well taken care of is the original nonstick surface. The holes in this porous metal fill with oil, and when hot, prevent food from sticking to the surface. These skillets should never be washed with soap, or they will need to be re**seasoned**—a process of heating the pan and rubbing oil into its pores to reestablish the nonstick surface. Cast iron is also great for even heat transfer and for remaining hot after food is placed in it. I often use my skillet directly on my outdoor grill for crisping up the skin on chicken or searing a piece of tuna.

Immersion blender

An immersion blender is also referred to as a stick blender or by a TV chef as a "boat motor." It is an electric blender that is attached to a wand and can be submerged in a bowl or pot for blending. It's a great tool that will save you the cleanup of your countertop blender as well as the need to transfer things to and from the blender in batches. You can find immersion blenders in the kitchen supply section of most larger discount stores, often for less than twenty dollars.

Portable electric fryer

You do not need a dedicated fryer to deep-fry at home, but it sure makes the process easier. Fryers allow you to remove your oil from the stovetop, and they prevent you from getting the oil dangerously hot by keeping it at a consistent temperature. They come with a basket that fits the fryer and hangs above the oil for easy draining. Look for the largest capacity one you can find at a price that is reasonable to you. The more oil you have, the less the temperature of the oil will drop when you put cold food into it. The hotter your oil stays, the better your food will be.

Coffee grinder

Many people today grind their own coffee beans for a fresh-tasting cup of coffee. Why not grind your own spices for fresher tasting food? Whole spices keep much longer than preground ones do and are easy to grind yourself. A small, home coffee grinder is great for this purpose. Do not use the same grinder for coffee as you do spices—unless you want spiced coffee.

Mortar and pestle

If you don't want to buy a coffee grinder and feel the need to connect with your ancestors, use a mortar and pestle. This tool is great for grinding, crushing, and turning things into pastes. Sure, they take a bit more elbow grease than electric appliances, but they allow you more control over the finished product.

Pasta machine

A pasta machine is a tool that can roll dough incrementally from about a quarter of an inch to a very thin sheet. They often come with attachments that will help you further shape your dough by cutting it into different sizes and shapes. A pasta machine allows you to get pasta and other doughs thin quickly—without breaking your back with a rolling pin. Electric and hand-cranked models are available. The choice is yours, but I prefer a hand-cranked model for my kitchen because I think pasta tastes better when my arm hurts from cranking.

Mandolin

A mandolin is a cutting device with a very sharp blade or blades. It is often adjustable and allows for quick, uniform cutting of firm vegetables and fruits. A mandolin is also handy for slicing items very thinly. You can find stainless-steel, professional models for a couple hundred dollars, but plastic ones with interchangeable blades are available at a fraction of the cost.

Blowtorch

Most importantly, blowtorches are cool. I am a big fan of fire, especially when you can hold a lot of it in your hand. Blowtorches are handy for making crème brulee, crisping the skin of fish or poultry, and browning the outside of meats. Go for an industrial-strength one instead of a model you would find in a fancy kitchen store. The kitchen store model just doesn't have the firepower to get jobs done quickly (and it's not as fun). You can pick up a more powerful one at your local hardware store. Hopefully this is obvious, but use in a well-ventilated area and not around any combustible materials.

Food mill

A food mill works by forcing food through a particular size plate with holes in it. You crank the handle to push food through the holes, making food smooth and removing skins, seeds, and fibrous material. Food mills are great for mashed potatoes and applesauce and for straining thickened soups. They are available in just about any kitchen supply section.

Instant-read thermometer

This invaluable little tool allows you to test the doneness of foods without having to guess or cut into the item. It is a small thermometer that you insert directly into the center of a dish to find an accurate temperature in a matter of seconds. An instant-read thermometer is great on large pieces of meat or seafood and even with baked goods.

Candy/frying thermometer

Candy/frying thermometers typically have a temperature range from 100 to 400 degrees. You can use them to tell the temperature of very hot sugar or oil for frying. Look for a thermometer with readings for both candy and frying so that you only have to buy one. Also look for models with clips on them so that you can hang them onto the side of a pot and into your frying oil.

Stand mixer

A powerful stand mixer is a great tool to have in the kitchen. It is small enough to sit on your countertop, and it comes with a number of attachments—typically a dough hook, a paddle, a whip, and a mixer bowl that will hold around five quarts, depending on the model. Optional accessories include meat grinders, sausage stuffers, and juicers. Stand mixers can be pretty expensive, but they will save you a lot of elbow grease and time.

Small wares

A number of other items are great to have around the kitchen, and they all come in various shapes and sizes. In my opinion, the most important factor is that they feel good to you and do your job well. For tongs and spatulas, I like ones made of metal that are strong enough to last without getting deformed. Before buying, attempt to bend them on the shelf of the store. (Don't tell them I told you to do this.) If you can bend the tool, it won't work the way it should. Don't get tricked into buying ones that have all sorts of extras, like knife blades and bottle openers attached to them. Buy high-quality, basic ones. Besides, you should have a bottle opener permanently attached near your grill anyway.

For rubber scrapers or spatulas, always get high-heat models that are less likely to melt into your food as you cook. They work just as well as the others for mixing cold items, so there's no need to have both.

It's also a good idea to have a meat mallet. If you don't, you can use a sauté pan for some things, as well as a hammer designed for hitting nails. However, a designated meat mallet is safer in the dishwasher and is easier to work with.

Measuring tools

Eventually you may be able to measure most things by eye without the aid of measuring tools. Even so, it's a good idea to have a set of measuring cups and spoons handy. A liquid measurer made of clear glass or plastic with amounts delineated on the side is also good to have. When baking, exact weights can be important, as some dry ingredients shouldn't be measured in measuring cups because their weight may vary depending on how compacted the cup of ingredient is. The more compacted the ingredient is in the cup, the more it will weigh. This is especially important when making large amounts of baked goods. For these situations, a small scale is useful and can be the difference between a good baked item and a great one.

How to Use This Book

Whenever cooking from a recipe, read the entire thing before you even step foot into your kitchen. Make sure you understand what you need, what you are going to do, and how you are going to do it. This is part of your *mise en place*, or getting ready to cook. You want everything in its place, so that when you begin cooking you don't have to stop because you don't understand or you forgot to buy or prepare something.

Each recipe in this book has a story that accompanies it. Some describe how I came up with the recipe or where I stole the idea from. Others speak of places I worked or how family members influenced a particular recipe. Some simply tell you why I think the recipe is cool. You'll also find interesting, food-related quotes and general cooking tips throughout the recipes. All the chef tips are listed in the appendix D in the back of the book.

All of the temperatures listed in the book are in Fahrenheit. There is a conversion table in the back of the book if you need to know temperatures in Celsius. All the amounts are listed in the English system. You'll also find a metric equivalency table in the back of the book to help with these conversions.

In appendix C, you'll find a guide to converting recipes to higher and lower total amounts. All of the recipes can be cut in half or doubled without any changes. Most can be converted to any other amount without any worry, either. A few will require some common sense, a larger pan than the recipe calls for, or cooking things in smaller batches.

The abbreviations used in this book are pretty standard. A number of times I use t.t., which represents "to taste" and is usually used for final seasoning. In these cases, add a little of the seasoning and then taste. If you think it needs more, add it.

Other abbreviations

pnch.	pinch	c.	cup
cl.	**clove**	pt.	pint
t.	teaspoon	qt.	quart
T.	Tablespoon	gal.	gallon
lb.	pound	oz.	ounce

All listed cooking times are approximate. I can probably do some of these recipes faster than you can, and somebody else can do them faster than me. If you're very methodical and like to take it slow, you may want to add a few extra minutes. All of the cooking times also assume proper *mise en place*. Before actually beginning to cook, ensure that you have all of the ingredients and equipment needed and that any prep that needed to be done beforehand is complete. The more efficiently you can work, the faster and better your results will be. While the cooking times listed include prep times, some do not include times for inactive or variable things such as when items need to be brined or marinated. More detail for these procedures and times is included in specific recipes.

Don't be a slave to the recipes. Use your imagination. Play with your food. If you don't like an ingredient, leave it out or substitute something similar. With the exception of baked goods, don't worry about measuring everything perfectly. If the red pepper you bought yields 1 1/4 cups and the recipe only calls for 1 cup, just use it all. If you forgot to buy carrots at the store, don't let that stop you from making something; just try it without.

My hope is that you love these recipes and never use another cookbook again. I know that's unrealistic, but I had that goal in mind when writing this book. Each of these recipes is wicked good to me and my family and friends. Don't be afraid to change them to make them wicked good for you and yours.

Before we get to the recipes, one more note: this book is meant to be used and abused. In a few months, I hope that it's stained, dirty, highlighted, and earmarked. It should smell a bit funny and have a loose binding. You can try to preserve it by photocopying items to keep the book out of the kitchen or by wrapping it in plastic wrap once open to your recipe. Remember that it's a cookbook, not some rare collector's item. Write your own notes in the margins, cross out ingredients if you didn't like them, and change amounts if you like more or less of something. The whole idea is to have fun and make your cooking and eating experiences personal, not just a recreation of what I like.

Appetizers and Snacks

This was probably my favorite part of the book to write and test. I love flavorful little bites of food that are easy to eat just about anywhere. You can serve most of the items in this section as small portions at a cocktail party or when watching a game with friends. You can also make them into larger portions and serve as entrées.

In this section, you'll find dips listed first. Each comes with a recommendation on what to use to dip, but just about anything will work—especially your finger. Be creative in your use of these dips. Try putting them on a burger or warming them up and tossing them with some leftover pasta.

In the middle of this chapter are several items focusing on seafood. I enjoy good seafood but don't crave it very often, so I was surprised at the number of recipes using seafood that ended up in the book. Most of these are great items for the seafood beginner because they don't have strong flavors or odors.

Toward the end of this section is my recipe for ultimate chicken wings, which are great all by themselves. Following this are recipes for ten different sauces to toss the wings in. Try serving a few different ones and letting your guests choose how to sauce the wings themselves. Create your own new sauces by combining different sauces together.

You'll even find a couple dessert-inspired entries here. These are not so sweet that they need to be served only for dessert. They even work great as little snacks at a party, or you can make them into larger portions and serve them as dessert all by themselves.

"Food is our common ground, a universal experience."
—James Beard

Appetizers and Snacks Contents

Buffalo Chicken Dip

Credit for this recipe has to be given to Paul Frade, a former student of mine. This kid put hot sauce on literally everything. One day I challenged him to come up with a dish that he could bake in the oven, and he created a buffalo chicken dip. I've tweaked the recipe a bit, but it's in the spirit of what he created.

Using breaded chicken is important to the consistency of the dish, but store-bought chicken or even restaurant leftovers work just as well as frying the chicken yourself.

This recipe will yield about 4 cups of finished dip and take you about 25 minutes total.

Ingredients:
1 c.   cream cheese
1 c.   cheddar cheese spread (such as Wispride)
1 c.   bleu cheese dressing
1/4 c.   hot sauce
1 stalk celery, diced fine
8 oz.   chicken fingers, cut into bite-size pieces

Combine all the ingredients except the chicken in the bowl of a small mixer, and mix using a paddle until combined.

Fold in the chicken by hand. **Bake** at 375 degrees in an ovenproof dish of your choice until bubbling and beginning to brown, about 10 minutes.

Serve warm.

You may also use a microwave to heat the dip, but you will lose any flavor developed through browning.

"Never eat more than you can lift."
—Miss Piggy

Baked Cheese Dip

This dip is loaded with cheese and has a nice bite from barely cooked garlic. The addition of mayonnaise keeps it from getting too stringy. It's great with or without the artichokes. You can also try substituting some small, cooked shrimp or scallops for a fun twist from the sea. For another fun snack, you can also spread the dip on bread and bake the two together.

This recipe will make about 5 cups of finished dip and take about 25 minutes total.

Ingredients:

1 c.	cheddar cheese, **grated**
1 c.	pepper jack cheese, **shredded**
1 c.	Parmesan cheese, grated
1 c.	mayonnaise
1	onion, small, chopped fine
2 cl.	garlic, minced
6 oz.	artichoke hearts, chopped
	bread, crackers, or tortilla chips for dipping

In a medium mixing bowl, combine all the ingredients.

Add to a small baking dish, and **bake** at 350 degrees until the dip begins to bubble, about 15 minutes. Serve warm.

Chef Tip: Keep Your Cutting Board Still
Place a dampened paper towel under your cutting board before beginning to work. This will prevent it from sliding around while you cut.

Pizza Dip

Ahh, pizza dip. This is the dish people most often ask me to make when I'm invited to a party. When I lived in Colorado, I was pigeonholed into making pizza dip any time I left the house. Sure, I could bring some creative "chef thing," just as long as I brought the pizza dip.

The inspiration for this recipe came from the pizza dip my Aunt Pam would bring to parties. It's probably the simplest and tastiest thing in this book. When put on a cracker or bagel chip, it actually tastes like you're eating pizza. Try it on a burger or just baked on some pizza dough.

This quick recipe will yield about 5 cups of dip and take you about 10 minutes to make.

Ingredients:
1   12-oz. block extra-sharp cheddar cheese, **shredded**
1   28-oz. can diced tomatoes, drained
1 T.   Italian seasoning

In a microwave-safe bowl, combine all the ingredients.

Microwave in 45-second intervals, stirring after each, until the dip is warm and the cheese is only beginning to melt.

Do not allow the dip to overheat, or the cheese will melt together in a stringy mess (which still tastes great!).

Chef Tip: Don't Store Food in the Refrigerator
Okay, well there are lots of foods that you should keep in the refrigerator, but dry foods, such as crackers, croutons, and chips, are not among them. The refrigerator is a very humid place and will make items such as these grow stale quickly. It's better to tightly wrap or use a clothespin to pinch the item closed. Then, keep in a cool, dry place.

Mexican Pizza Dip

This is a takeoff on pizza dip created for a Mexican-themed party. I was a bit nervous to bring it when people were used to the original, but everybody loved it, especially with tortilla chips or baked pita chips. The two dips have the same basic ingredients, but the Mexican version has some extras.

This recipe will make about 5 cups of finished dip in about 10 minutes.

Ingredients:

1	12-oz. block extra-sharp cheddar cheese, **shredded**	
1	24-oz. can diced tomatoes, drained	
1 T.	oregano, dry	
1 t.	cumin	
1 t.	freshly ground black pepper	
1	12-oz. can black beans, drained	
2	limes, juiced	
t.t.	hot sauce	

In a microwave-safe bowl, combine all the ingredients.

Microwave in 45-second intervals, stirring after each, until the dip is warm and the cheese is only beginning to melt.

Do not allow the dip to overheat, or the cheese will melt together in a stringy mess.

"People who drink light 'beer' don't like the taste of beer; they just like to pee a lot."
—Capital Brewery, Middleton, WI

Spinach Artichoke Dip

The first time I had a dip like this—chunks of chicken mixed with cheesy-spinachy goodness—it changed my idea of what a dip could be. For this recipe, I've left out the chicken but kept all the other goodness in its simplest form. Enjoy with crackers, pretzels, or **crostini**, or serve it in a bread bowl.

If you want to try it with chicken, just add a pound of cooked, sliced chicken breast or even a few roughly chopped, frozen chicken fingers.

This recipe will make about 5 cups of dip in about 20 minutes.

Ingredients:
1	onion, large, diced
2 T.	butter
12 oz.	cream cheese
1	14-oz. can artichokes, drained and lightly chopped
1	9 oz. package frozen spinach, thawed and squeezed dry
t.t.	**kosher salt** and hot sauce

In a large sauté pan, lightly **sauté** the onion in butter until soft.

Turn heat to medium, and add the cream cheese. Stir until melted.

Add spinach and artichokes, and mix well.

Taste and adjust with salt and hot sauce.

Remove from heat, and serve warm for easy dipping.

Chef Tip: Hold Your Knife Properly
When using a knife, wrap your hand around the handle or pinch the blade with your thumb and forefinger. Do not cut with your index finger extended on the top of the knife. Over time, this will cause pain up into your forearm.

Baked Brie with Homemade Crostini

This dish, often seen at fancy restaurants or parties, is actually super easy to make. I really like the way the sweet acidity of the marmalade complements the creaminess of the cheese. Use your imagination, and top it with anything you like to eat, or make it with only the cheese and pastry. Remember to play with your food!

This recipe will make 1 wheel of baked brie and plenty of **crostini** to eat that cheese on in about 30 minutes.

Ingredients:

1	8-oz. wheel brie
1 sheet	**puff pastry**, thawed
8 T.	orange marmalade
2	eggs
1/2 c.	milk
	Crostini (recipe follows)

Roll out the puff pastry until it's about twice the size of the brie.

Brush the pastry with butter, and spoon the marmalade in the center of the pastry.

Place the brie upside down in the center of the pastry.

Pull the corners of the pastry over the cheese until they barely overlap.

Trim any excess. (Excess can be used for decoration.)

Place on a sheet pan, and brush with an **egg wash** made by stirring together the eggs and milk.

Bake at 425 degrees for 10 minutes or until golden brown.
Serve warm on crostini.

Crostini

Ingredients:
1 loaf   French bread
1/2 lb   butter, melted or extra virgin olive oil
t.t.   kosher salt

Slice bread about 1/4" thick. Lightly brush with butter, and sprinkle with salt. Bake at 250 degrees until crispy.

Allow to cool.

Hummus and Homemade Pita Chips

Making your own hummus is quick, easy, and much cheaper and tastier than buying it at the store. The chips described below are the best-tasting pita chips I've ever had, and I've never found anything close on a store shelf. The basic idea for the chips is from a chef I worked with at a large conference center. It didn't matter how many chips we put out, we always ran out. Hopefully his healthy snack will leave you wanting more too.

The hummus will take about ten minutes to make and will yield 2 1/2 cups. The pita chips will take about 25 minutes to make and will result in plenty of chips for the hummus recipe.

Ingredients:

2 cl.	garlic
3 T.	extra virgin olive oil
1	15-oz. can chickpeas, drained
1/4 c.	**tahini**
6 T.	lemon juice, preferably fresh
1 t.	honey
	water, as needed
t.t.	freshly ground black pepper
t.t.	kosher salt
	pita chips (recipe follows)

In a food processor, puree the garlic with the olive oil.

Once pureed, add the chickpeas, tahini, lemon, and honey. Puree until smooth.

Add water to adjust the consistency, if desired.

Season with salt and black pepper.

Serve on pita chips.

Pita Chips

4	pita pockets, 10" or so diameter
2 T.	water
2 T.	extra virgin olive oil
pnch.	freshly ground black pepper
pnch.	garlic powder
pnch.	onion powder
1 t.	**kosher salt**
1 T.	honey
1/2 t.	curry powder

Using a small knife, cut around the edge of the pita bread and separate it into 2 full-size halves. Cut into the desired shape and size, and place rough side up on a sheet pan.

In a small mixing bowl, combine the remaining ingredients and brush or drizzle on the pita pieces.

Bake at 250 degrees about 15 minutes or until crispy and beginning to brown.

Store in a cool, dry place—not the refrigerator.

Chef Tip: Peel and Mince Garlic
Before peeling fresh garlic, cut off the dried-out end of the clove that's attached to the rest of the head. Then, place it on a cutting board and, with you knife sideways atop the garlic, tap lightly to loosen the skin.
Once peeled, repeat the same motion with the knife on the garlic, now hitting the clove hard enough to smash it. If you need it finer, simply chop or mash against the cutting board a little at a time with the edge of the knife. Adding a bit of salt while mashing will help the garlic mash even faster; salt works as sandpaper does.

Bleu Cheese Puffs with Grilled Pear

This is another recipe that I created for a cooking class I was teaching. I had to match food to different martinis. The martini that went with this has long been forgotten, but this great and simple recipe lives on.

This recipe will make about 20 puffs in about 20 minutes.

Ingredients:
2   ripe pears
1/2 lb.   bleu cheese
1 can   crescent rolls
1/4 lb.   butter

Peel the pears, and slice into strips about 1/2" square.

Place on a hot grill to allow grill marks to form.

Slice the crescent rolls into 1/2" slices. Flatten slightly with your hand.

Brush the dough with butter, and place one piece of pear and about 1/2 t. of bleu cheese on it.

Roll the dough, leaving a seam on the bottom.

Place on a sheet pan and **bake** at 375 degrees about 5 minutes or until golden brown.

Chef Tip: Butter vs. Margarine

Margarine is cheaper than butter, but that's about all it has going for it. Unless a recipe specifically calls for margarine, use butter. It's more flavorful, melts better, browns better, and is richer than margarine. Never mind the fact that butter is simply churned cream with no added chemicals or hydrogenation.

In a pinch, margarine is an okay substitute, but use the real stuff when you can. It makes a difference.

Mini Beef Wellingtons

These little appetizers are technically not beef Wellingtons, but they follow the basic idea and are the name sounds cool. I made these up for a repeat conference guest who was bored with the past items on our banquet menu. These were made up quickly using things we had in the kitchen, but were such a big hit that we put them on our menu.

This recipe will yield about 30 appetizers in about 20 minutes.

Ingredients:
1 lb.   beef tenderloin, cleaned, cut into 1 1/2" strips
t.t.   **kosher salt**
t.t.   cracked black pepper
3 T.   Dijon mustard
          phyllo dough, as needed
1/2 lb. butter

Season the beef with salt and pepper, and brown it in a hot pan or on a grill.

Lightly cover the beef with mustard.

Brush the phyllo dough with butter, and wrap the beef in the dough. (The amount of dough will vary depending on the size of meat you use, but you want a finished thickness of at least 10 layers of dough.)

Brush the outside of the dough with butter.

Bake at 375 degrees until medium rare, about five minutes.

Allow to rest three or four minutes. Slice into pieces about 1" long and serve.

Chef Tip: Resting Meats

Any time you roast or grill meat, let it rest before serving—not because it's tired but because when it comes out of the oven or off the grill, the outside is much hotter than the inside. Resting will allow these temperatures to even out a bit and will actually allow larger pieces of meat to finish cooking by another few degrees. Once rested, the meat will release much less of its juice when it's cut.

Crab Rangoons with Ginger Dipping Sauce

These are a must-order anytime my friends and I order Chinese food, but they are relatively easy to make at home as well. I tend to like a hint of sweetness in mine, but omit the sugar if you desire.

You can freeze these before cooking for up to a month with no problem. They will just take about half a minute longer to cook from a frozen state.

This recipe will make about 40 rangoons, depending on how full you stuff them. It will take about 30 minutes to complete the rangoons and sauce.

Ingredients:

12 oz.	cream cheese
5 oz.	imitation crab, **shredded** by hand
1/4 c.	scallions, sliced fine
1 oz.	soy sauce
2 T.	granulated sugar
pnch.	freshly ground black pepper
40	wonton wrappers
	water
	Ginger Dipping Sauce (recipe follows)

Mix all the filling ingredients in a mixer with a paddle attachment until well combined.

Spoon 1 t. of filling onto each wonton wrapper.

Lightly wet two edges of each wrapper, and fold them to create triangle. Take care not to allow any filling to leak out.

Deep-fry at 350 degrees until golden brown and floating, about 2 minutes.

Serve with Ginger Dipping Sauce.

Ginger Dipping Sauce

3 c.	soy sauce
1 c.	honey
1 c.	**rice vinegar**
2 T.	fresh ginger, minced
½ c.	scallions, sliced

In a medium mixing bowl, combine all the ingredients.

If not using that day, refrigerate for later use.

Prosciutto-Wrapped Shrimp on a Rosemary Skewer

A chef and I created this recipe because we forgot to order the scallops for the bacon-wrapped scallops we were supposed to serve. You follow the same basic procedure but with totally different ingredients. You can use regular toothpicks to hold them together, but using the rosemary skewer makes for a more complex flavor.

This recipe will make about 12 portions of 2 shrimp each in about 20 minutes.

Ingredients:

24	shrimp, peeled and deveined, size 21–25 or so
25	prosciutto slices
9	rosemary sprigs, leaves removed (long, firm stems are preferred)
2 T.	extra virgin olive oil
1 T.	**kosher salt**
1 T.	freshly ground black pepper

In a mixing bowl, toss together the shrimp, oil, salt, and pepper.

Cut the rosemary sprigs into 3" sections.

Wrap each shrimp in a slice of prosciutto.

Skewer two shrimp on each rosemary section.

Bake at 375 for 8 minutes or until the shrimp are cooked.

Serve immediately.

Chef Tip: Shrimp Sizes

Shrimp are typically sold based on their size, which is determined by how many shrimp of a particular size it will take to equal a pound. For example, you'll find between 21 and 25 shrimp in a pound of 21–25 sized shrimp. The smaller the number, the larger the shrimp.

Once shrimp get really big, they stop being categorized by a range and are sized by how few make up a pound. If you see shrimp labeled U-12, there are fewer than 12 shrimp per pound. Shrimp that are U-6 would be twice the size of the U-12 shrimp.

Steamers

Steamers are my favorite snack food whenever I'm on Cape Cod. These subtly salty and meaty clams don't need any fancy seasonings—just some good-quality butter for dipping and an ice-cold beer for sipping.

It will take you about 10 minutes to make a heaping mound of steamers— enough for 2 or 3 people as an entrée or for 8–10 as appetizers or snacks.

Ingredients:
2 lb.   steamer clams, fresh, rinsed of sand
1/2 c.   water
1/2 lb.   butter, melted or **clarified**

Check clams to ensure that there are no open or broken shells. Discard any if found.

In a large pot with a tight-fitting lid, gently add the clams and water.

Cover tightly and allow to cook over high heat until all the clams have begun to open, about 4–6 minutes.

Remove the clams from the liquid, and strain the **broth** with a fine **strainer**.

Serve hot with melted butter and clam broth for dipping.

"An empty stomach is not a good political advisor."
—Albert Einstein

Steamed Mussels

I'm definitely a steamer clam guy, but these mussels are a great change of pace from time to time. I like to add more flavorings to the mussels than I use on the steamers, but I'm still careful not to overpower the flavor of the mussels.

These are great served with some crusty bread or large croutons to sop up the liquid.

It will take you about 10 minutes to make a heaping mound of mussels—enough for 2 or 3 people as an entrée or for 8–10 as appetizers or snacks.

Ingredients:

2 lb.	live mussels, debearded and rinsed
2 T.	butter
3 T.	**shallots**, chopped
1 cl.	garlic, chopped fine
2 T.	fresh parsley, chopped
3/4 c.	white wine (whatever you like)
t.t.	**kosher salt**
t.t.	freshly ground black pepper

In a large pan, **sauté** the shallots and garlic in butter for 1 minute.

Add all the remaining ingredients and **simmer** covered until all the mussels open.

Pour the mussels and liquid into a serving bowl and serve.

Chef Tip: How to Debeard a Mussel
Oftentimes mussels have thin filaments coming out of their shells to which seaweed and other items from the sea may stick. Remove these "beards" by pulling them off with your fingers. It's also always a good idea to wash and lightly scrub mussels before cooking to remove anything else sticking to the shells.

Rhode Island Style Fried Calamari

What makes this Rhode Island style calamari is the sweet and spicy vinegar sauce. It goes great with calamari and is also awesome on an Italian grinder.

This recipe will yield enough calamari for about 8 people as a snack in 15 minutes or so.

Ingredients:

1 lb.	calamari, tentacles and tubes cut to about 1" wide
2 c.	milk
3 c.	**clam fry** or flour seasoned with salt and pepper
3 c.	**rice vinegar**
3/4 c.	granulated sugar
2 T.	canned diced hot cherry peppers or 1 T. of crushed red pepper flakes
2 t.	**kosher salt**
1/2 c.	water

Soak the calamari in milk until you're ready to fry.

In a medium saucepan, combine all the sauce ingredients and **simmer** 2 minutes.

Remove the calamari from the milk, and **dredge** in flour to coat evenly.

Fry at 350 degrees for about 1 minute, until floating and just beginning to brown.

Remove from the fryer, and allow to drain briefly.

Toss with sauce and serve.

"Anyone who eats three meals a day should understand why cookbooks outsell sex books three to one."
—L. M. Boyd

Shrimp Dumplings

These tasty appetizers also make a healthy snack. A couple of students and I created them for an Asian-themed dinner run by high school students that our school did for 250 people. Much to the chagrin of the students, the homemade dough had to be rolled out by hand just as you would pasta sheets for ravioli. It took the kids hours to get enough of it rolled out for four hundred dumplings. I promise it won't take you as long.

This recipe will take about 1 hour to make 30 dumplings, depending on their size.

Ingredients:

1 1/2 c.	water, **boiling**
3 c.	flour
1 T.	**kosher salt**
20	shrimp, medium size, completely peeled, deveined, and diced
1	egg white
1 t.	ginger root, minced
1 t.	garlic, minced
2 T.	scallions, diced fine
3 T.	soy sauce
1 t.	honey
1 t.	**kosher salt**
	Nonstick pan spray

In a medium mixing bowl, combine the flour and water, and mix until firm dough is formed. Allow the dough to rest for at least 20 minutes.

In a medium mixing bowl, combine all the remaining ingredients except the pan spray.

Using a pasta machine, roll out to #5. Or, roll as thinly as possible by hand.

Cut the dough into 3" squares, and place about 2 t. of filling on each square.

Bring all four corners together, and press to seal along the seams.

Lightly spray the dumplings with nonstick spray to prevent them from sticking to each other.

Steam 5–7 minutes or until the shrimp is cooked.

Serve with the same ginger dipping sauce as found with the crab rangoon recipe on page 17.

Oysters Rockefeller

This is my twist on the classic baked oyster dish purportedly named for John D. Rockefeller because these oysters, too, are very rich. I love adding Pernod or another licorice-flavored liqueur to balance some of the richness.

This recipe will yield 18 oysters in about 30 minutes.

Ingredients:

18	oysters, opened on half shell, liquor reserved
3 oz.	butter
2	**shallots**, diced fine
1 cl.	garlic, minced
3 c.	fresh spinach, picked of stems (frozen can be used but must be squeezed dry)
1/2 c.	Pernod (Sambuca or Anisette may be used)
1/4 c.	heavy cream
1/2 c.	bread crumbs
1/2 c.	Parmesan cheese
t.t.	salt and pepper

In a sauté pan over medium high heat, melt the butter and **sauté** the shallots and garlic for 2 minutes. Add the spinach and cook until wilted.

Add the Pernod, cream, and reserved oyster liquid. Allow to **simmer** for 3 or 4 minutes.

Remove from heat, and add bread crumbs and Parmesan cheese. Mix well.

Adjust the seasoning with salt and pepper.

Arrange the oysters in a single layer on a sheet pan and spoon the mixture evenly over all oysters.

Bake at 450 degrees for about 10 minutes. Serve hot.

Chef Tip: How to Open an Oyster

Oysters are best opened using an oyster knife, which may look similar to a paring knife but has a thicker blade and a blunt point at the tip. While firmly holding the oyster in a thick rag (so you don't stab yourself if you slip), insert the tip of the knife into the small hole at the pointed end of the oyster. Apply a bit of pressure, and use a twisting action to break the seal of the oyster. Once opened, run your knife along the top of the shell to detach the oyster. Be careful to keep the oyster level to prevent any of the flavorful juice (liquor) from getting out.

Scallop and Bacon Flatbread

The base for this dish is pizza dough, which my local supermarket just so happens to do a great job of making. And they don't leave a mess in my kitchen! When making pizza, don't get too stressed about spreading the ingredients on evenly. The different proportions of ingredients on each slice will help make every bite unique.

This recipe will make one large flatbread that will feed 10–12 people as an appetizer or 4 people as an entrée pizza. It should take about 40 minutes to make.

15	cherry tomatoes
pnch.	salt
pnch.	granulated sugar
1 lb.	dough, pizza or bread
2 T.	extra virgin olive oil
6 oz.	scallops, about ½" each (larger ones work fine too)
3/4 c.	bacon, cooked, chopped
3 T.	chives, chopped
1/2 c.	feta cheese (a nice goat cheese is great too)
pnch.	**kosher salt**
pnch.	freshly ground black pepper

Cut the cherry tomatoes in half and place on a sheet pan, cut side facing up. Sprinkle lightly with salt and sugar. **Bake** 7–10 minutes at 400 degrees.

Roll out the dough to 1/4" thickness.

Coat the dough with olive oil.

Place the dried tomatoes and all other remaining ingredients onto the dough.

Bake at 400 degrees 12–15 minutes, until the crust is golden brown.

Cut into the desired size and serve warm.

Chef Tip: Cook Bacon

It's fine to cook bacon on a stovetop in a pan if you're doing a small amount, but if you have to cook lots of it, bake your bacon. Line a sheet pan with some parchment paper, and bake at 375 degrees until the bacon is cooked how you want it. Once done, you can just take the bacon off with some tongs and cook another batch.

While you're at it, try tossing you bacon in some brown sugar before baking it. Now that's a tasty treat!

Potstickers

This recipe is a bit more complex than many of the others in this book, but I think the end result is worth it. You may substitute ground chicken, ground turkey, or ground shrimp for the pork with great results.

They are called potstickers because they literally stick to the pan when you begin to cook them. Don't worry about that, though; they'll release from the pan by the time they're done.

This recipe will make about 30 dumplings in approximately 30 minutes.

1 lb.	ground pork
1/2 c.	scallions, chopped finely
1/4 c.	bell pepper, diced finely
2	eggs, lightly beaten
2 T.	Worcestershire sauce
1 T.	brown sugar
1 T.	**kosher salt**
1 t.	freshly ground black pepper
1/2 t.	cayenne pepper
1 t.	fresh ginger, minced
2 T.	soy sauce
30	wonton wrappers
	water, as needed
	vegetable oil, as needed
1 qt.	chicken **stock**, as needed

Combine the first eleven ingredients (up through soy sauce) in a mixing bowl.

Place about 1 t. filling in the center of each wonton wrapper. Using a wet finger, wet two sides of the wrapper and fold corner to corner to make a triangle. Press the seam with your finger to seal tightly.

In a hot sauté pan, add enough oil to cover the bottom of the pan, and then add enough potstickers to cover the pan. Do not move, as this is the time the food sticks to the pan.

Allow to cook until browned (about 90 seconds).

Add 1 c. chicken stock, and cover immediately. Use caution, as on a gas stove a flame up may result when you add stock.

Allow to cook about 3 minutes or until the pork is cooked.

Serve with ginger dipping sauce found with the crab rangoon recipe on page 17.

Fried Artichoke Hearts with Roasted Red Pepper Aioli

This recipe for aioli uses a couple of shortcuts to make it a bit easier for the home cook to prepare. If you feel up for a challenge, you can make fresh mayonnaise to use for the base of the aioli or you could even start with fresh artichokes for frying.

These bite-size hors d'oeuvres are a crisp, tasty alternative to the boring cocktail party foods most of us are used to. Don't feel that you have to wait for an upscale get-together to eat these; they go just as well with football and a cold beer as with a martini and a tuxedo.

This recipe will make 24 artichoke hearts and ample aioli for dipping in about 20 minutes.

Ingredients:

	Vegetable oil for frying
6	artichoke hearts, quartered
2 c.	flour
1/2 c.	milk
2	eggs
2 c.	bread crumbs
1/4 c.	Parmesan cheese, **grated**
1/4 c.	fresh parsley
pnch.	**kosher salt**
pnch.	freshly ground black pepper
	Roasted Red Pepper Aioli (recipe follows)

Place the flour in small bowl.

In a separate bowl, combine the milk and eggs.

In a third bowl, combine the remaining ingredients.

Pass the artichoke hearts through the flour bowl, egg bowl, and bread-crumb bowl.

Deep-fry the breaded artichoke hearts at 350 degrees until golden brown, about three minutes.

Allow to drain briefly, and then serve with Roasted Red Pepper Aioli.

Roasted Red Pepper Aioli

Ingredients:

2 c.	mayonnaise
1 T.	lemon juice
1 t.	garlic, pureed into paste
1	red pepper, roasted, peeled, and seeded
pnch.	**kosher salt**
pnch.	freshly ground black pepper

Combine all the ingredients for aioli in a food processor until well mixed.

Store in the refrigerator for up to two weeks.

Savory Goat Cheese and Walnut Cheesecake with Figs

This is not a traditional cheesecake in that it is not sweet but savory and is meant to be served as an appetizer. The creamy tartness of the cheese combined with the bitterness of the walnuts and the sweetness of the figs makes for a great blend of flavors. These tasty hors d'oeuvres may seem pretty complicated, but they're actually quite simple to make.

This recipe will make about 30 cheesecakes in 30 minutes.

Ingredients:

4 oz.	cream cheese
3 1/2 oz.	goat cheese
1	egg
1/4 c.	walnuts, chopped
1 T.	chives, chopped
pnch.	black pepper
30	wonton wrappers
1 c.	figs, chopped fine
	nonstick pan spray, as needed

Combine all the ingredients except the wonton wrappers and figs in a mixer using a whip attachment. Mix until smooth.

Spray both sides of the wonton wrappers with nonstick pan spray. Place in a muffin tin as if making tiny cups.

Add 1/2 t. of chopped fig to the bottom of each cup.

Fill cups 2/3 of the way with the cheese mixture.

Bake at 350 degrees about 10 minutes, or until the cheese puffs up and the wonton is browned.

"Avoid fruits and nuts. You are what you eat."
—Jim Davis, "Garfield"

Oven-Dried Roma Tomatoes with Goat Cheese, Bacon, and Chives

The key to these tasty little appetizers is the tomatoes. They are baked at a relatively low temperature so that they dehydrate a bit, but they don't become bitter as completely dried tomatoes often do. They have an intense flavor and a soft texture that work great with the smooth cheese and crunchy bacon.

This recipe will make 25–30 pieces in about 45 minutes.

Ingredients:
12	Roma tomatoes, halved lengthwise
t.t.	**kosher salt**
t.t.	sugar
1	5-oz. package goat cheese
4	bacon slices, cooked and crumbled
4	chives, cut into 1" lengths

Arrange the tomatoes on a cookie sheet, cut size up. Lightly sprinkle with salt and sugar.

Bake at 300 degrees for about 20 minutes, or until soft and beginning to dehydrate.

Remove from the oven and cool.

Once cool, spoon about 2 t. of cheese, 1 t. of bacon and 2 pieces of chive on top of each tomato.

Chef Tip: Cut Goat Cheese

Goat cheese tends to stick to a knife when you cut it, making it difficult to get nice, clean slices. Next time, try cutting it with a piece of dental floss. You'll love the results.

Beef Tenderloin Crostini with Boursin Cheese and Caramelized Onion

These versatile little snacks can be served warm or cold. I usually like them cold, but have served them warm if I am making them last minute. Be sure to spread the cheese on the **crostini** before adding the beef or onion. The cheese will act as an insulator to protect the crunchy bread from any moisture in the other ingredients.

This will make about 20 appetizers in about 60 minutes, but a lot of that is inactive time.

Ingredients:

1/2	French bread loaf
4 T.	extra virgin olive oil
t.t.	**kosher salt**
t.t.	freshly ground black pepper
1 lb.	beef tenderloin, cleaned
1	5-oz. package **Boursin** garlic and fine herbs cheese
1	large onion, **julienned**
¼ lb.	butter

Slice bread into 20 or so bite-size pieces. Lightly brush with oil and season with salt and pepper. **Bake** in a 300-degree oven until just crispy, about 15 minutes.

Season the beef with oil, salt, and pepper. **Grill** or **roast** until medium rare, about 125 degrees on an **instant-read thermometer**. Allow to cool in the refrigerator. Slice thinly.

Sauté the onion in butter seasoned with salt and pepper until caramelized.

On each piece of crostini, spread about 1 t. of Boursin, lay down one piece of beef, and cover with a few pieces of caramelized onion.

Chef Tip: Grilling

The first step in planning a menu or dish that requires a grill is to make sure you have fuel. Whether using gas or charcoal, you can't get very far without anything to burn. This may sound obvious, but I hear stories about people running out of gas right in the middle of a cookout. Don't let that be you!

Texas Toast Sliders

Sliders or mini-burgers have become all the rage at restaurants lately. They also make the perfect two-bite appetizer or snack. These sliders stand up tall because they're made with Texas toast, which is extra thick cut bread, and they are held together nicely with frilled toothpicks. The mayonnaise plays an important role in protecting your bread from getting soggy, and that extra bit of fat adds a lot of flavor. I think these are near perfect as is, but go ahead and experiment with sauces or other toppings you usually enjoy on burgers.

It will take about 30 minutes to make 16 mini-burgers.

Ingredients:

½	onion, finely diced
3 T.	water
1 lb.	ground beef (I use 80/20, but use what you like)
t.t.	**kosher salt**
t.t.	freshly ground black pepper
6	slices of **Texas toast**, crust removed and cut into fourths
½ c.	butter
½ c.	mayonnaise
16	dill pickle slices
4	American cheese slices, cut into quarters

Add the onions and water to a sauté pan over medium heat, and cook until the onions are **translucent**. Do not allow them to caramelize.

Roll the ground beef to a thickness of about 1/4".

Place on a preheated griddle or sauté pan, season with salt and pepper, and cook until medium well.

Remove from the pan, and cut into 10 mini-burgers.

Add 1 piece of cheese to each piece of meat.

Meanwhile, lightly brush the bread with butter and brown in a sauté pan or griddle over medium heat. (Use the same pan or griddle if there is enough room.)

Spread a thin layer of mayonnaise on each piece of toast.

Place the cooked burger and cheese on the toast.

Add one pickle slice to each burger.

Add a pinch of onions to each burger.

Top with the remaining piece of toast.

Ultimate Chicken Wings

I like my chicken wings crispy on the outside with some sort of breading that isn't too thick. The breading is important because it gives the sauce something to stick to, but I hate it when a restaurant serves a wing that actually has more breading than chicken. This recipe uses a **brine** to add some extra flavor and moisture to the wings before they're breaded. That is followed by what I think is the perfect breading. The wings come out best when fried, but **baking** them isn't all that bad, either—just not quite as crispy.

This recipe will yield a bunch of wings, but the total all depend on their size. It will be enough to feed 10 or so people as an appetizer, but if this is all you're going to eat during the game, they will feed only 2–3 people. They will take about 30 minutes to make not including the time they spend in the brine.

Ingredients:

2 lb.	chicken wings, any size, cut however you prefer them
1/2 gal.	water, warm
1/2 c.	lemon juice
1/2 c.	**kosher salt**
1/2 c.	granulated sugar
4 c.	flour
3 T.	kosher salt
4 t.	freshly ground black pepper
4 t.	onion powder
4 t.	garlic powder
2 t.	**confectioners' sugar**
	vegetable oil for frying

In a large pan, combine the water with the lemon juice, salt, and granulated sugar. Stir until dissolved.

Add the chicken wings and let set, refrigerated, from at least 1 hour up to overnight.

Meanwhile, prepare the breading by mixing all the ingredients to combine.

Drain the brine from the wings.

Transfer the wings to a large mixing bowl and add half of the breading to the wings. Toss to coat.

Allow to sit 10 minutes or so to allow the flour to become wet from the moisture in the chicken.

Add the remaining flour, and toss to coat.

Fry in small batches at 350 degrees until fully cooked. To check doneness, cut into the largest wing to ensure that there's no remaining pink.

Cooking time will vary depending on the size of wing used, but it will range from about 6–10 minutes.

Chicken Wing Sauces

Following are 10 quick and easy sauces that you can toss with your wings to give them a different twist. In addition, just about any of the other sauces found in this book go great with chicken wings, especially sauce used in General Gau's Chicken on page 123.

Traditional Buffalo Sauce

Ingredients:
3 c.   Frank's RedHot
2 c.   butter, melted
½ c.   lemon juice

In a medium mixing bowl, combine all the ingredients.

I like Frank's for this recipe because it is the brand used in the original buffalo wing sauce.

New and Improved Buffalo Sauce

Ingredients:
1 T.   garlic, fresh, minced
4 oz.   butter, melted
1 c.   Frank's RedHot
1 oz.   lemon juice
2 oz.   honey
3 oz.   sour cream
1 t.   kosher salt
1 t.   freshly ground black pepper
1 t.   cayenne pepper

In a medium mixing bowl, combine all the ingredients.

Keep refrigerated.

Teriyaki Sauce

Ingredients:
1 t.	garlic, fresh, minced
1 t.	ginger, fresh, minced
1 c.	**hoisin sauce**
1/2 c.	soy sauce
1 T.	honey

In a small saucepan, **simmer** all the ingredients for 3 minutes.

Honey Lime Cilantro

Ingredients:
4 T.	cilantro, chopped
1 c.	lime juice, fresh
5 T.	honey
1 t.	**kosher salt**
1 t.	freshly ground black pepper

In a medium mixing bowl, stir all the ingredients to combine.

Parmesan Peppercorn

Ingredients:
1 c.	Parmesan cheese, **grated**
2 T.	coarsely ground black pepper

As soon as the wings come out of the fryer, toss them in a bowl with the cheese and pepper. The cheese will melt and stick to the wings and take the pepper with it.

Honey Barbecue

Ingredients:
2 c.	your favorite barbecue sauce
1/2 c.	honey

In a medium mixing bowl, stir all the ingredients to combine.

Lemon Pepper

Ingredients:
2   lemons, **zested** and juiced
1 T.   coarsely ground black pepper
1 t.   **kosher salt**
1 t.   granulated sugar

Bring all ingredients to a **simmer** in a small saucepan.

Simmer 2 minutes.

Garlic Herb

Ingredients:
1/2 lb. butter
3 T.   fresh garlic, minced
2 T.   fresh parsley, chopped
1 t.   oregano, dry
1 t.   thyme, dry
1 t.   freshly ground black pepper

In a small saucepan, melt the butter.

Add the remaining ingredients and allow to simmer for 5 minutes, stirring occasionally.

Honey Mustard

Ingredients:
2 oz.   yellow mustard
2 oz.   mayonnaise
5 t.   honey
pnch.   **kosher salt**
pnch.   freshly ground black pepper

In a medium mixing bowl, stir all the ingredients to combine.

Asian Peanut Sauce

Ingredients:
2 c.	peanuts
1/2 c.	soy sauce
1/2 c.	honey
1/2 c.	**rice vinegar**
1 c.	water
1 T.	ginger, fresh, chopped
4 t.	peanut butter

Combine all ingredients in a blender, and blend until smooth.

Chef Tip: Hot Sauce

There are hundreds upon hundreds of hot sauces available for purchase, none better than any other. Don't be afraid to taste-test some and choose a favorite. Brand names that are listed in recipes are not important; just use your favorite.

The basic ingredients in hot sauce are hot peppers and vinegar. If you ever find yourself with excess peppers, puree them, pour in some white vinegar, and you have your own hot sauce. Play with the flavors by adding herbs, garlic, different vinegars, or a combination of peppers.

Apple and Brie Puffs

I developed this recipe for a class that I taught about small, simple, and yummy cocktail party items. The buttery, soft brie works well with the apple and melts beautifully, but any cheese will do. Try topping the puffs with caramel sauce for more of a dessert feel.

This recipe will make about 20 puffs in around 20 minutes.

1 sheet	**puff pastry**, thawed
1/2 lb.	butter, melted
2	apples, peeled, seeded, and diced into 1/3" cubes
1	brie wheel, cut into 1/4" cubes

Roll the puff pastry until about 1/8" thick. Cut into 2" squares.

Brush both sides of the puff pastry squares with butter.

In the center of each square, place one piece of apple and one piece of brie.

Fold the sides of the dough over, and place on a sheet pan so that the seam is on the bottom.

Bake at 400 degrees for 7–10 minutes or until the pastry is golden brown.

"Any fool can count the seeds in an apple. Only God can count all the apples in one seed."
—Robert Schuller

Chocolate Caramel Popcorn

This is the recipe I used in my first tryout video to be on *The Next Food Network Star*. I'm not sure what they didn't like, but it certainly wasn't this recipe. Packaged in small tins, this has been a favorite holiday gift ever since I started making it. You can even store it in the freezer, well wrapped, for up to a month.

This recipe will make enough for a large bowl of popcorn to feed about 10 people as an appetizer and will take about 30 minutes to make

Ingredients:
1 c.   unpopped popcorn
2 c.   granulated sugar
1/2 c.   water
1 lb.   semi-sweet chocolate, in small pieces
1/4 lb.   butter

Pop popcorn as directed on the package. (Microwave popcorn works just fine, and the added butter and salt are a nice bonus.)

In a large pan, combine the sugar and water. Stir just to dissolve the sugar. Place over high heat and allow to cook until the sugar reaches caramel color. Be very careful, as caramel is extremely hot! (Time depends on the size of your pan and power of your stove. You know you're getting close when the bubbles start to get larger in size.)

Turn off the heat and add the popped popcorn to the pan. Stir to coat all the popcorn in the caramel. Pour onto a cookie sheet lined with **parchment paper**. Allow to cool at room temperature while preparing chocolate.

In small saucepan, melt the butter. Add the chocolate and allow to melt. Pour over cooled caramel corn. Place in freezer until the chocolate sets.

Chef Tip: Caramel

Caramel in its simplest form is granulated sugar that has been heated to between 320 and 350 degrees and develops a caramel aroma, flavor, and color. Once heated to this stage, it can be made into sauces, brittles, or candies, or even formed into shapes. The temperature of caramel is about the same as the oil in a deep-fryer. It burns just as bad too, and will stick to you if you touch it, so use extreme caution.

Soups, Chilies, and Salads

This section of the book started out as soups and salads, but apparently I like chili a lot more than I like salads. I have since changed the title of this chapter. Chili isn't really a soup, but I didn't want to include recipes for it in the entrée section either because chili is so often used as a starter or as part of an appetizer such as potato skins or loaded French fries. There are four different chilies I wanted in the book, so I just made this chapter soups, chilies, and salads.

The recipes are listed in just that order. They begin with gazpacho, a cold vegetable soup, and continue with other vegetable-based soups. Then we move into more hearty and meaty soups. As you'll probably soon realize, these are the type of soups I like best—ones that warm you on a cold winter day and are bold enough to be eaten all by themselves for dinner.

Following the hearty soups are the chilies. You'll find a pretty healthy and tasty all-vegetable chili, a relatively standard chili, a unique chili that I entered into a competition, and finally a chili that is loaded with flavor and heat from pork and green chilies rather than beef and tomatoes.

Finally, I've included one salad that makes for a great starter to a meal and is well worth trying. After that I've listed some great recipes for making your own dressings and croutons. Using these simple recipes, buy the greens and vegetables you like best and go nuts!

"Wish I had time for just one more bowl of chili."
—Last words of Kit Carson

Soups, Chilies, and Salads Contents

Gazpacho

This gazpacho makes a great summertime meal with nothing but a couple of hunks of good, crusty bread. Because you're serving the vegetables in their natural state with no cooking and very simple seasonings, freshness is a must. You can make this gazpacho any time of year, but it's best when the produce used is in season locally.

This recipe will make about 2 ½ quarts of soup or enough to serve 6–8 people a bowl before a meal. It should take about 20 minutes to make.

Ingredients:

1 T.	fresh garlic, minced
2 T.	**kosher salt**
3 lb.	tomatoes, fresh
1 lb.	bell peppers
1 lb.	cucumbers, peeled and seeded
4	scallions (white and green)
1/2 c.	fresh parsley, chopped
5 T.	extra virgin olive oil
3 T.	sherry vinegar (or any other vinegar you like)
3 c.	tomato juice
2 t.	hot sauce
t.t.	freshly ground black pepper

Rough chop all the vegetables. Remove 2 c. of vegetables for garnish.

Puree all the ingredients in a blender or food processor. Serve ice cold.

Garnish with the 2 c. of chopped vegetables you saved earlier.

"Don't eat until you're full; eat until you're tired."
—Hawaiian saying

Roasted Red Pepper Soup with Cilantro Cream

Made almost completely from fresh vegetables, this flavorful recipe is very low in fat. I first made this soup while working at a hotel outside of Dallas. We actually served it in a bowl with the roasted red pepper soup on one side and a black bean soup on the other side. When both soups were ladled into the bowl at the same time, a sort of yin-and-yang symbol was created. When topped with cilantro sour cream from a squeeze bottle, it looked amazing. That said, this soup also does just fine on its own.

This recipe will make about 10 cups of soup and feed 4–6 people when served before a meal. It will take about 45 minutes to make, although you can save a great deal of time by roasting your peppers the day before.

Ingredients:

6	red bell peppers
4 T.	vegetable oil
1 c.	carrot, **rough chopped**
1 c.	onion, rough chopped
1 c.	celery, rough chopped
4 c.	vegetable **stock**
1 T.	**kosher salt**
t.t.	hot sauce of your choice
	Cilantro Cream Sauce (recipe follows)

Lightly coat the red peppers with oil, and **roast** in a 375-degree oven until the skins blister and the flesh is soft.

Wrap the peppers in plastic wrap or place them in a plastic bag. Allow to cool.

While cooling, **sauté** the carrot, onion, and celery with the remaining oil until the onions are **translucent**.

Add the vegetable stock, and allow to **simmer** until the carrots are very soft.

While the soup is simmering, remove the skin and seeds from the roasted peppers.

Add the peppers to the soup and puree with an immersion blender.

Adjust the seasoning with salt and hot sauce.

If you want a finer consistency for your soup, strain it after cooking.

Top with the cilantro cream sauce.

Cilantro Cream Sauce

1 c.   sour cream
2 T.   cilantro, chopped fine
1 t.   **kosher salt**
1/2 t.   hot sauce

Combine all of the ingredients in a small mixing bowl.

Store in refrigerator for up to two weeks.

Cream of Tomato Soup

I grew up dipping heavily buttered strips of toast into bowls of canned tomato soup, and I loved every minute of it. It wasn't until I went to culinary school that I found out that cream of tomato soup was not just for kids or people looking for a quick meal; it can be a real gourmet treat as well as a total comfort food if done well. The flavors built by **aromatic** vegetables, the acidity of the tomatoes, and the smoothness of the cream all **simmering** together are tough to beat.

This soup will take 35–40 minutes to make and will yield a bit over 2 quarts of soup, or enough for 8 or so portions.

Ingredients:
1	onion, **rough chopped**
2	carrots, peeled and rough chopped
3	celery stalks, rough chopped
1/2 lb.	butter
1	6-oz. can tomato paste
1 1/4 c.	flour
1	26-oz. can diced tomatoes
1/2 gal.	chicken **broth**
1 pt.	heavy cream
t.t.	**kosher salt**
t.t.	coarsely ground black pepper

In a large sauce pot over medium heat, **sweat** the onions, carrots, and celery in butter for 5 minutes.

Add the tomato paste, and cook 5 minutes to remove some acidity.

Add the flour and cook 5 more minutes, stirring frequently to prevent anything from sticking to the bottom of the pan. You are now making a **roux**.

Add the tomatoes and chicken broth, and stir frequently until the soup **simmers**.

Simmer 5 minutes or until the carrots are soft.

Remove from heat, and puree using an immersion blender.

Return the soup to the burner, and add cream, salt, and pepper.

Strain the soup when done for a smoother texture.

Chef Tip: Tomato Paste

Tomato paste is essentially tomato concentrate. It's full of flavor and color but is very acidic right from the can. Always be sure to cook items with tomato paste, as the heat will reduce the acidity over time.

Butternut Squash Bisque

This tasty soup uses vegetables traditionally available in the fall and winter. It contains almost no fat and is quite easy to make. I often serve this soup at the beginning of our Thanksgiving meal. Want to add a little something extra? Just before eating, lightly whip some heavy cream with a touch of powdered ginger and add a dollop to each bowl. It melts into the soup, adding a wonderful creaminess.

Substituting some parsnips for some of the carrots or **roasting** your vegetables before putting them into the pot are a couple ways to develop even more flavor in this simple, healthy soup.

This recipe will take about 25 minutes to make and will serve 8–10 people a bowl of soup each.

Ingredients:

3	celery stalks, **rough chopped**
1/2 lb.	carrot, rough chopped
1	onion, rough chopped
1 qt.	apple juice
2 c.	chicken or vegetable **stock**
1 lb.	butternut squash, peeled and rough chopped
2 c.	water
t.t.	kosher salt
t.t.	hot sauce

Combine all ingredients in a sauce pot. **Simmer** until all the vegetables are tender.

Puree using an immersion blender.

Adjust with salt and hot sauce.

For a finely textured soup, run through a fine **strainer** to remove any bits of vegetable not totally pureed.

"I went on a diet, swore off drinking and heavy eating, and in 14 days, I lost 2 weeks."
—Joe E. Lewis

Roasted Sweet Onion Cream Soup

This soup was invented out of boredom. I was working at a conference center and was tired of the soups we typically made. The roasted onions we had leftover from lunch served as my inspiration. After a bit of experimentation, this recipe was the result. Any time I got people to order this off a menu, they would ask me how to make it. So here you go!

This recipe will make about 2 1/2 quarts of soup or enough to feed 8–10 people a large bowl of soup. It should take approximately 45 minutes.

Ingredients:

5	onions, sliced
1/2 c.	butter, melted
1 c.	honey
2	celery stalks, **rough chopped**
1 c.	butter
1 c.	flour
3 pt.	chicken **broth**
1 pt.	cream
t.t.	**kosher salt**
t.t.	freshly ground black pepper

On a sheet pan, toss the onions with the honey and 1/2 c. of melted butter. **Roast** at 350 degrees, stirring occasionally, until the onions turn golden brown, about 20 minutes. Be careful not to let the edges burn, or the soup will be bitter

In your soup pot, **sweat** the celery in the remaining butter over medium heat for 5 minutes.

Add the flour, reduce the heat to low, and cook 7–10 minutes to make a **roux.**

Add the roasted onions to the pot.

Add some of the chicken broth to the sheet pan, and stir to **deglaze** any flavor on the pan.

Add what you're deglazed and the remaining chicken broth to the soup, and bring to a **simmer**.

Using an immersion blender, puree the soup until smooth.

Add cream, and adjust the seasonings with salt and pepper.

If desired, strain for finer consistency.

Cream of Chicken Soup

For me, this is the ultimate in a comfort food soup. It has everything a basic chicken-and-vegetable soup has, but the slight thickening and the addition of cream create a velvety texture that makes you feel warm inside.

This recipe will make a bit over 2 quarts of soup or enough to serve 8–10 portions. It should take about 25 minutes to make.

Ingredients:
1/2 c.	vegetable oil
1/2 c.	butter
1 lb.	chicken, diced
1	large onion, finely diced
2	celery stalks, finely diced
2	carrots, finely diced
1 c.	flour
1/2 gal.	chicken **broth**
1 pt.	heavy cream
1 t.	hot sauce
t.t.	kosher salt

Add the butter and oil to a large preheated pot. Add the chicken, and allow to brown.

Add all the vegetables, and **sweat** for 3 minutes.

Reduce the heat, add the flour, and cook 5 more minutes.

Whisk the chicken broth into the pot.

Bring to a **simmer,** stirring frequently to prevent sticking

Add the heavy cream and hot sauce.

Adjust seasonings, if necessary, with kosher salt and hot sauce.

Chef Tip: Stock vs. Broth

Broth is the liquid left over from simmering meat, fish, or vegetables in water. Stock is a bit more complex in that it is a mixture of vegetables and bones with seasonings such as peppercorns, bay leaves, and parsley stems, all simmered in water. Ingredients for stock can be roasted to produce a darker and more flavorful product.

If a recipe calls for stock, broth is an acceptable substitute and vice versa.

Hot and Sour Soup

Whenever I have to choose a soup at a Chinese restaurant, this is my pick. I can't think of any other soup that is so far from our soup "norms" but still tastes great. The combination of acidity from the vinegar with the bite of ginger and a touch of heat from hot sauce make this perfect to eat while tailgating, just before heading into a cold football game.

This recipe will make about 3 quarts of soup or enough to serve 10–12 people. It should take about 30 minutes.

Ingredients:

1/2 lb.	chicken or pork, ground
1 c.	onion, diced
1 c.	mushrooms, sliced
3 T.	ginger, fresh, minced
1 T.	garlic, fresh, minced
1/2 c.	scallion, sliced thinly
2 oz.	soy sauce
2 oz.	rice wine vinegar
1/2 gal.	chicken **broth** or **stock**
2 oz.	hot sauce
3–4	**wood ear mushrooms**
	cornstarch slurry
2	eggs, lightly beaten

Soak the wood ear mushrooms in hot water for 20 minutes. Strain and rinse.

Meanwhile, brown the meat in a large preheated pot. Add the onions, and cook until **translucent**.

Add the ginger and garlic, and cook for 1 minute.

Add the remaining ingredients except the cornstarch slurry and eggs. Bring to a **simmer**.

Add enough slurry to achieve the desired thickness (should coat the back of a spoon).

Rinse the wood ear mushrooms in cold water, and add to the soup.

Pour the beaten eggs on top of the soup, and stir once. (The heat of the soup will instantly cook the eggs.)

Serve hot.

Sausage and Potato Soup

I created this Sausage and Potato Soup completely with leftovers at a restaurant I worked at. We had baked potatoes, Italian sausage, and sautéed onions and tomatoes left over from our lunch meal. I basically just put them all in a pot with some chicken stock and a couple other things, and let it **simmer**. After it was finished, the staff and I sat around the kitchen dipping crusty French bread into our bowls of soup.

This recipe will make about 3 quarts of soup or enough for 10–12 bowls in 20–25 minutes.

Ingredients:

1 1/2 lb.	Italian sausage, cooked
1/4 c.	extra virgin olive oil
1	onion, diced
1 T.	garlic, fresh, minced
1	28-oz. can diced tomatoes
1/2 gal.	chicken **broth**
3	baked potatoes, cooked and **rough chopped**
1 T.	fennel seed, lightly toasted
t.t.	freshly ground black pepper
t.t.	**kosher salt**

Heat a **heavy gauge** sauce pot over high heat. Add the oil and sausage, and **sear** the sausage.

Add the onion, and cook 2 minutes.

Add the garlic, and cook 1 minute.

Add all the remaining ingredients, and allow to simmer 10 minutes.

Adjust the taste with salt and pepper.

Cream of Wild Mushroom and Roasted Garlic Soup

My inspiration for this recipe came from a soup I had to make every day when I worked at the Don Cesar Resort in St. Petersburg Beach, Florida. It's a pretty basic cream of mushroom soup but with the addition of roasted garlic. The smooth sweetness of the garlic works great with the earthiness of the mushrooms, and the richness of the cream makes me want to eat mushroom soup again.

This recipe will make about 3 quarts of soup or enough for 10–12 portions in about 30 minutes.

Ingredients:

12 cl.	garlic, peeled and trimmed of dry ends
1 c.	vegetable oil
2 lb.	mushrooms, rinsed (any variety will work)
1	onion, **rough chopped**
2	celery stalks, rough chopped
2	bay leaves
1 1/2 c.	flour
2 qt.	chicken **stock**, cold
1 pt.	heavy cream
t.t.	**kosher salt**
t.t.	freshly ground black pepper

In a small ovenproof dish, **roast** the garlic at 375 degrees, submerged in oil, until tender.

Meanwhile, on a sheet pan, roast the mushrooms 10 minutes to intensify their flavor.

Pour the oil from the garlic into a large sauce pot on high heat, and **sweat** the onions and celery until the onions are **translucent**.

Add the roasted mushrooms, garlic **cloves**, and bay leaves, and cook 2 more minutes.

Lower the heat to medium low, and stir in the flour. Cook 6 minutes to create a **roux**.

Stir in the cold chicken stock and bring to a **simmer,** stirring frequently.

Puree using an immersion blender.

Return the soup to the burner, add cream, and adjust the taste with salt and pepper. If the soup is too thick, add chicken stock until you reach the desired consistency.

Strain the soup for a more velvety texture.

Smoked Chicken Corn Chowder

The first time I had a soup like this was atop a mountain on a cold day teaching skiing in Vail, Colorado. It warmed me up and left me wanting more. The following days, my roommates were more than happy to test my different versions of it until I found one I was happy with. The smoky flavor comes from the chicken and, to a lesser extent, the bacon. If you can't make or get smoked chicken, use unsmoked chicken and add a teaspoon of **liquid smoke** to the soup.

This recipe will make about 3 quarts of soup or enough for 12 portions. It should take about 35 minutes to make.

Ingredients:
6	bacon strips (raw), diced
1/2 lb.	butter
1 lb.	chicken, diced
1	onion, diced
2	celery stalks, diced
4	baby red potatoes, skin on, diced
16 oz.	corn kernels, fresh or frozen
1 t.	thyme
1 1/2 c.	flour
1 1/2 pt.	chicken **broth**, cold
1 pt.	heavy cream
t.t.	**kosher salt**
t.t.	freshly ground black pepper

In a large pot over medium high heat, **render** the bacon until crispy.

Add butter. Once melted, add the chicken and allow to brown.

Add the onion, celery, potatoes, corn, and thyme, and cook until the onions are **translucent**.

Reduce the heat to low, add the flour, and cook 6 or 7 minutes to make a **roux**.

Add the cold chicken broth, turn the heat to high, and whisk until the soup begins to **simmer**.

Once simmering, add cream and adjust the seasonings with salt and pepper.

Chef Tip: Remove Corn from the Cob

You can remove most of the corn by simply cutting it off the cob. Be careful not to cut too deeply into the cob, or you will end up with crunchy bits of cob mixed in with the corn. Once you slice off the kernels, hold your knife perpendicular to the cob and scrape downward. This will remove the rest of the flavorful insides of the kernels that you couldn't get off before.

Vegetable Chili

This is one of my dad's favorite dishes. It is very tasty and actually is good for you. Some in my family even prefer it over meat chili. There are tons of fresh vegetables in this chili, but none are necessary. If there is something that you do not like, replace it with something else or leave it out all together. The most time consuming part is preparing all the fresh vegetables, but you will be rewarded for your work by the great smells coming from your kitchen while it is **simmering**, and with a great tasting chili

This recipe will make about 1 1/2 quarts of chili or enough for 4 good size bowls. It takes a bit of time to prepare all the vegetables, but you should be able to get it done in about 20 minutes and before cooking another 40 minutes.

Ingredients:
3 T.   vegetable oil
1 c.   onion, diced
1 T.   fresh garlic, minced
1/2 c.   red pepper, diced
1/2 c.   green pepper, diced
1/2 c.   zucchini, diced
1/2 c.   yellow squash, diced
1/2 c.   corn kernels (fresh or frozen)
1/2 c.   carrot, diced
1/2 c.   mushrooms of your choice, sliced
1   15-oz. can black beans, drained
1   15-oz. can kidney beans, drained
2   28-oz. cans diced tomatoes in tomato puree
5 T.   chili powder
t.t.   hot sauce
t.t.   **kosher salt**

In a large pot, **sauté** the onions in oil until **translucent**.

Add the garlic, and allow to cook for 30 seconds.

Add the remaining fresh vegetables, and sauté about 5 minutes.

Add the beans, tomatoes, and chili powder. Allow to simmer for 30 minutes.

Adjust the seasoning with hot sauce and salt.

Camp Vail Chili

I developed this recipe while working at a Colorado day camp for children ages six to twelve. The kids and I were trying to come up with something to enter into a local chili contest. We never did enter it, but we did come up with this excellent basic chili recipe.

This recipe makes 1 1/2 gallons and can be converted into larger or smaller amounts with good results. It should take about 30 minutes to put together before cooking for another 45 minutes.

Ingredients:

2 1/2 lb.	ground beef (80/20 works well)
3	large onions, **rough chopped**
1 1/2 T.	freshly ground black pepper
2 t.	**kosher salt**
6 oz.	tomato paste
2	28-oz. cans diced tomatoes
2	15-oz. cans black beans, drained
2	15-oz. cans white beans, drained
2	15-oz. cans kidney beans, drained
7 t.	chili powder
1 T.	hot sauce
3 T.	sugar

Add the ground beef to a large preheated pot on high heat, and brown the meat.

Add the salt, pepper, and onions. Cook until the onions become **translucent.**

Add the tomato paste, lower the heat to medium, and cook for 10 minutes, stirring frequently.

Add all the remaining ingredients, and allow to **simmer** 45 minutes.

Adjust the flavor with hot sauce and kosher salt.

Chef Tip: Freeze Foods

Freezing items can be a great way to prepare a meal in advance or
to keep leftovers, but the freezer can also become the black hole of your
kitchen. Keep it organized by always labeling and dating what you put in
there. Also keep the oldest items in front so that you're more apt to use
them first and less apt to forget about them.

Your freezer should always run at 0 degrees or below. Just because water
freezes at 32 degrees doesn't mean that there isn't still some bacterial action
going on. Also try to use things as soon as reasonably possible. Food will last
a long time in the freezer, but the longer it's in there, the lower the quality
when you take it out.

Matt's Championship Chili

This is a chili that I created over a couple of months with the intention of entering it into a chili competition. It was my first contest like this, and I was literally the only one of twenty-two competitors without a tent—and it rained all day. I almost went home before setting up but decided to stick it out. I certainly didn't win for best booth, but this recipe won for best restaurant chili.

The recipe makes about 1 gallon and freezes well. It will take about 30 minutes to put together and 1 hour to cook. I hope you enjoy!

Ingredients:

4 oz.	bacon fat
1 1/2 lb.	ground beef
1 1/2 lb.	coarsely ground pork
5	onions, chopped
56 oz.	tomato juice
1/4 c.	molasses
1/4 c.	dark chili powder
3	limes, juiced
1	48-oz. can diced tomatoes with juice
2 T.	garlic, fresh, minced
1 oz.	**adobo** sauce
2 T.	cumin
2 t.	cayenne pepper
2 oz.	honey
2 oz.	white **masa harina**
t.t.	kosher salt
t.t.	freshly ground black pepper

In a large pan, brown the beef and pork with bacon fat.

Add the onions and cook until **translucent**.

Add all the remaining ingredients except the masa harina. **Simmer** 1 hour.

Add the masa harina to adjust the thickness.

Adjust the flavor with salt and pepper.

Pork Green Chili with Bacon

The first time I ever had a green chili was when I lived in Colorado. My buddy Ryan Doster and I decided to try and re-create the dish, but we didn't really know what made it green. We walked to this little supermarket in Denver looking for some green stuff that might go in a chili. We ended up buying some tomatillos and Anaheim peppers and a pound of bacon. Our attempt to copy the chili came out better than the original, and I've served it at Super Bowl parties ever since.

For those of us who grew up with red chili made with beef, this is quite a departure from the norm, but it's a trip worth taking.

This recipe makes around 3 quarts of chili and freezes very well. It will serve about 10 bowls and will take 50–60 minutes to make.

Ingredients:

1/2 lb.	navy beans, soaked
1 1/2 lb.	tomatillos, husks removed and rinsed
1 lb.	Anaheim or poblano peppers (or any other green chili pepper)
1/2 lb.	bacon, diced
1/2 c.	bacon fat
2 lb.	pork, coarsely ground or diced fine
2	onion, diced
1 T.	cumin
1 T.	honey
t.t.	**kosher salt**
t.t.	hot sauce

In a saucepan over medium heat, cook the beans with 4 c. cups of water until tender.

Place the tomatillos on a sheet pan, and **roast** at 375 degrees until mushy and lightly browned. Remove from the oven, and take off any brown skin with your fingers.

Meanwhile, lightly coat the peppers with vegetable oil and roast until the skins blister. Remove the skin, stems, and seeds from the peppers. Reserve the flesh and any juices.

In a food processor or blender, puree the tomatillos, peppers, and any liquid from roasting. Reserve.

In a large pot, **render** the bacon with bacon fat.

Once the bacon is crispy and the pan is very hot, add the pork. Allow to brown.

Add the onions, and **sauté** 3 minutes.

Add the pureed tomatillos and peppers, cooked beans, and all the remaining ingredients.

Allow to **simmer** 15 minutes.

Adjust the seasonings with salt and hot sauce to taste.

Grilled Pear Salad with Candied Walnuts and Gorgonzola

This salad has a little bit of everything: creaminess from the cheese, a touch of sweetness from the pears, and some crunch and bitterness from the walnuts. All of these ingredients complement one another and work well with any type of vinaigrette dressing. If you don't like Gorgonzola cheese, try substituting some goat cheese.

This salad will take about 30 minutes to prepare and about 3 minutes to put together. It will make enough for 8 salads.

Ingredients:

2	fresh ripe pears of your choice
1 ½ c.	walnuts
½ c.	brown sugar
2 T	water
1 t.	vanilla
1 c.	Gorgonzola cheese, crumbled salad dressing of your choice
8 c.	mixed greens

On a sheet pan, combine the nuts, sugar, water, and vanilla until the nuts are evenly coated.

Roast at 350 degrees about 6 minutes or until the sugar is bubbling.

Meanwhile, rinse the pears and remove the cores. Slice into desired size.

Place on a preheated medium-high grill, and **grill** until nice marks are achieved.

When done, remove the nuts from the oven, and allow the nuts to cool. Stir occasionally to loosen from the pan.

Toss the dressing, half of the candied nuts, and half of the cheese with the greens. Top the greens with pears and the remaining nuts and cheese.

"The only time to eat diet food is while you are waiting for the steak to cook."
—Julia Child

Basic Vinaigrette or Italian Dressing

In its simplest form, vinaigrette is vinegar and oil, often poured directly on lettuce greens. This recipe yields a more complex-tasting version that is simple to make. It was actually so popular that it became the house dressing at a restaurant I was chef at. Feel free to add or remove ingredients or change the type of vinegar or oil to suit your taste.

This recipe will make about 3 cups of dressing or enough to dress 12–20 salads, depending on their size and how much dressing you like. It should take about 10 minutes to make.

Ingredients:

1 c.	red wine vinegar
pnch.	**kosher salt**
pnch.	freshly ground black pepper
pnch.	garlic powder
pnch.	onion powder
1 t.	prepared mustard (the stuff from a jar)
1 T.	honey
pnch.	basil, dry
pnch.	thyme, dry
pnch.	oregano, dry
1 c.	Parmesan cheese, **grated**
2 c.	vegetable oil

Combine all the ingredients except the oil in a large mixing bowl, and mix until well incorporated.

Slowly add the oil while whisking.

"Cooking is like love; it should be entered into with abandon
or not at all."
—Harriet van Horne

Creamy Italian Salad Dressing

Creamy Italian Salad Dressing is one of my favorites. The addition of some mayonnaise to a basic vinaigrette dressing results in a creaminess and thickness that makes for a great dressing as well as a great dip.

This recipe will make about 3 cups of dressing or enough to dress 12–20 salads, depending on their size and how much dressing you like. It should take about 10 minutes to make.

Ingredients:

2 c.	mayonnaise
1 c.	red wine vinegar
1/3 c.	honey
2 T.	oregano, dry
2 T.	basil, dry
1 T.	thyme, dry
2 t.	fresh garlic, chopped finely
1 t.	onion powder
1/2 t.	**kosher salt**
pnch.	freshly ground black pepper
2 c.	vegetable oil

In a medium mixing bowl, combine all the ingredients except the oil.

While whisking the mixture, slowly add vegetable oil.

Refrigerate 2 hours to allow the flavors to combine before serving.

Cream Salad Dressing Base

This simple salad dressing base is like a mother sauce for creamy dressings. It's the foundation for three of the dressings in the book and countless others. You can easily double or triple the recipe. If you want to make the Ranch, Bleu Cheese, and Parmesan Peppercorn dressings all at the same time, make one large batch of the base and then divide it before you add the other ingredients.

All of the dressings that follow will keep up to 3 weeks if refrigerated and well wrapped.

This recipe makes about 4 cups of base and should take about 5 minutes to put together. The finished dressings yield around 5 cups or enough for 15–20 salads.

Ingredients:
2 c.   sour cream
2 c.   mayonnaise
1/4 c.   lemon juice
1 T.   onion powder
2 t.   **kosher salt**
2 t.   garlic powder
1 T.   freshly ground black pepper

Using a whisk, mix all the ingredients in a large bowl.

<u>Ranch</u>

4 c.   Cream Salad Dressing Base
1/2 c.   scallions, sliced fine
2 t.   dill weed, dry

Using a whisk, combine all the ingredients in a large bowl.

Bleu Cheese

4 c.   Cream Salad Dressing Base
2 c.   bleu cheese of your choice

Using an immersion blender, puree the dressing base and 1 c. of the bleu cheese.

Crumble the remaining bleu cheese, and stir into the dressing.

Parmesan Peppercorn

4 c.   Cream Salad Dressing Base
1/2 c.   Parmesan cheese, **grated**
1 T.   cracked black pepper

Using a whisk, combine all the ingredients in a large bowl.

Greek Salad Dressing

This super simple, super good dressing is quick to make and will last for weeks in the refrigerator. It is great on salads, but I like to crumble up some feta cheese and toss with this dressing and use as a dip with pita chips.

This recipe makes about 3 cups of dressing or enough for about 12 salads and will take about 10 minutes to put together.

Ingredients:
2 c.	mayonnaise
1 c.	apple cider vinegar
3/4 c.	honey
6 T.	oregano, dry
2 T.	water
1/2 t.	**kosher salt**
pnch.	freshly ground black pepper
2 c.	vegetable oil

Combine all ingredients but the oil in a mixing bowl.

Slowly add the oil while whisking. Allow to sit at least 30 minutes before serving to allow the flavors to combine.

Homemade Croutons

Homemade croutons rule! They are also a great way to use up excess or stale bread. Croutons are relatively simple to make and will keep for a week or so in a cool, dry place.

This recipe will make about 6 cups of finished croutons, depending on how big the loaf of bread you start with is. It should take about 45 minutes total to make.

Ingredients:
1   white bread loaf
1/2 lb.   butter
1 T.   fresh garlic, minced
1 T.   onion powder
1/2 T.   **kosher salt**
1 T.   freshly ground black pepper

Melt the butter in a medium saucepan. Add the garlic, onion powder, salt, and pepper. Allow to **simmer** 5 minutes.

Dice the bread, and place in a large mixing bowl. Pour the butter mixture over the bread and toss well.

Bake at 250 degrees until crispy and slightly brown, about 25 minutes.

"Good bread is the most fundamentally satisfying of all foods; and good bread with fresh butter, the greatest of feasts."
—James Beard

Entrees

This is the meat and potatoes of the book. Well, I guess potatoes are in a completely different section and this section includes a bunch of seafood and even some vegetarian entrées, but you get the idea.

When most of us sit down for a meal, we eventually expect to see one of these items. They are the main course and are often served with a vegetable and a starch. You'll find recipes for the veggies and starches in the next chapter.

We begin this section with a few vegetarian items—not because it's cool to be a vegetarian, but because they are all wicked good food. They don't necessarily count as "health food," but you can pretend they do if it will get you to try them.

These few items are followed by a bunch of seafood recipes. Once again, I ended up with a lot more seafood recipes than I expected. Rest assured that beginning seafood eaters will find some great recipes, as will the pros.

Finally we come to the meat: chicken, beef, and pork. I don't think any of these recipes would be on the eating plan of a dieter, but man do they taste good. And you know what they say … everything in moderation (especially country-fried steak), The way I figure, it's awfully healthy to smile—and that's just what these recipes make me do.

"Cookery is not chemistry. It is an art. It requires instinct and taste rather than exact measurements."
—Marcel Boulestin

Entrée Contents

Vegetable Lo Mein

Unfortunately, I've never been able to get a job cooking in a Chinese restaurant, so I just kind of made up this recipe on my own … and it's pretty darn good. The key to making this **lo mein** is to have all your *mise en place* (prep) ready, along with a very hot pan. If the pan is and stays hot, all the vegetables will retain their crispness and the sauce will dissolve and **evaporate** in less than 5 minutes.

This recipe will make 4 portions and should take about 30 minutes to make.

Ingredients:

1/2 lb.	noodles of your choice
1/2 c.	low-sodium soy sauce
3 T.	honey
2 T.	vegetable oil
1 t.	fresh ginger, minced
1/2 c.	carrot, peeled and sliced thinly
1/2 c.	snow peas, trimmed
1/2 c.	red pepper, diced
1/4 c.	scallions, sliced thinly
1/2 c.	bean sprouts
1/2 c.	mushrooms of your choice, sliced
1/2 c.	baby corn
1 t.	garlic, minced

In a large pot with **boiling** water, cook the noodles until **al dente**.

In a mixing bowl, combine the soy sauce and honey.

Get a **wok**-style pan or a large sauté pan very hot.

Add oil. (It may smoke a bit, but that's okay.)

Quickly add the ginger, followed by all the vegetables. Allow to cook until the vegetables begin to soften.

Add the garlic.

Add the noodles, and stir to coat with oil.

Add the soy sauce mixture a little at a time until the desired color and flavor are achieved. You may find you like it a bit less salty and don't add all the soy mixture.

Feel free to add or subtract vegetables or to add a half-pound of chicken, pork, shrimp, or whatever you're in the mood for.

Butternut Squash Ravioli

I cheat a little bit when making this recipe, but nobody seems to care much. Instead of taking the time to make pasta dough, I use wonton wrappers, which are thinner than the dough in most ravioli but work just fine. This dish is great tossed with some **brown butter** and a couple fresh sage leaves torn into a few pieces.

A former student of mine, Corey Bunnewith, suggests adding a pecan to each piece of ravioli for a different texture or lightly pan-frying the ravioli before tossing with whatever sauce you choose. I consider both of these to be wicked good ideas!

This recipe takes about 30 minutes to make and will yield 30 or so pieces of ravioli. That's enough for 4–6 portions.

Ingredients:
1/2 lb.   butternut squash, peeled and **rough chopped**
2 oz.   butter
1 T.   **kosher salt**
t.t.   freshly ground black pepper
          instant mashed potatoes, as needed (if filling is too loose)
30 .   wonton wrappers
          egg wash, as needed

Cook squash until very tender in **boiling** salted water.

Combine all the ingredients in the bowl of a mixer fitted with a whip attachment. Mix until smooth.

The texture should be similar to mashed potatoes. If it seems too thin, add some of the instant mashed potato as a thickener.

Lay out 15 wonton wrappers on your work surface.

Spoon 1 t. of filling on each wrapper.

Using a pastry brush or your finger, wet all 4 edges of the wrappers with egg wash.

Place the other wrappers on top of the filling, and press together to seal the edges.

Drop ravioli in a pot of boiling salted water for 4 minutes, remove with a slotted spoon, and serve.

Homemade Macaroni and Cheese

Macaroni and cheese is pretty much my all-time favorite meal. I have to admit that when cooking for myself, I've been known to make the stuff from the box—and I do enjoy it. This recipe, however, blows away the box version. I like a thick, creamy sauce that gets lots of its flavor from cheddar, a bit of bite from some Swiss, and a great texture from American cheese. To me, the best part of this recipe is the whole pieces of cheese that are put on top of the crumbs and start to brown on the edges as they cook in the oven—simply little pieces of heaven. I hope you enjoy this dish as much as I do.

This recipe makes enough for 10 large portions, which make great leftovers, and should take about 40 minutes to make.

Ingredients:

1 1/2 lb.	pasta of your choice (I like mini penne or cavatapi)
1/4 lb.	butter
1/2 c.	flour (heaping)
1 1/2 qt.	chicken **stock**, cold
30 oz.	Extra-sharp cheddar cheese, **grated**
8 oz.	Swiss cheese of your choice, grated
16	American cheese slices
t.t.	**kosher salt**
t.t.	hot sauce
1	sleeve Ritz-type crackers, crushed
2 oz.	butter, melted
pnch.	kosher salt
pnch.	freshly ground black pepper
pnch.	garlic powder
pnch.	onion powder
6 oz.	Extra-sharp cheddar cheese, sliced about 1/4" thick

In a large pot, with boiling salted water, cook the pasta until **al dente**. Drain.

In a medium pot, melt the butter over medium heat.

Add the flour, and stir consistently for 5 minutes to create a **roux**.

Raise the heat to high, add cold chicken stock, and stir until the mixture comes to a **simmer** and thickens.

Once thickened, turn off the heat and slowly add all of the cheese, stirring as it melts.

Taste and adjust the seasoning with salt and hot sauce.

In a mixing bowl, combine the crackers with the butter, salt, pepper, garlic powder, and onion powder.

Toss the hot cheese sauce with the drained pasta. Pour the mixture into individual bowls or a baking dish.

Cover with crumbs.

Evenly place the slices of cheese on top of the crumbs.

Bake at 350 degrees until the edges are bubbling and the cheese is beginning to brown, about 12 minutes.

Allow to cool briefly before serving so that the sauce with thicken a bit.

Chef Tip: Use Hot Sauce as Pepper

I often choose to use my favorite hot sauce in the place of black or white pepper in a dish. Not only does the hot sauce bring more complex flavor to the dish, but more importantly, it dissolves quickly and cannot be seen. Next time you make a soup or a sauce, try adding some hot sauce where you would use pepper, and then judge the results for yourself.

Haddock en Papillote

Cooking something *en papillote*, or in paper, is a great way to retain the natural flavors of a food and can also be quite healthy, as the method actually **steams** food inside your oven. This tasty dish contains no fat and stays nice and moist.

This recipe makes 4 portions and will take 20–25 minutes to make.

Ingredients:

4	haddock fillets, 6–8 oz. each
8	tomato slices
16	fresh basil leaves
t.t.	**kosher salt**
t.t.	freshly ground black pepper

Cut four pieces of parchment paper into heart shapes that are approximately twice the size of the fish.

Season the fish liberally with salt and pepper.

Place a piece of fish on one side of each heart-shaped paper.

Arrange 2 slices of tomato and 4 basil leaves on each piece of fish.

Fold the other half of the parchment paper over the fish.

Beginning at one corner of the paper, make small folds to seal together the outer edges. Continue until your paper package is completely sealed.

Bake at 400 degrees until the fish is done, about 10–14 minutes, depending on the size of the fish.

To serve, cut a slit in the top of the paper. Keep the fish in the paper for serving.

Potato-Wrapped Sea Bass with Tarragon Cream Sauce

The potato wrapping on this fish brings a crispy, flavorful, and colorful twist to what is otherwise a basic recipe. The Tarragon Cream Sauce is the perfect complement to the light delicate flavor of the fish.

This recipe makes 3 or 4 portions and should take about 30 minutes to make.

Ingredients:

1 lb.	sea bass, cut into pieces about 3" wide
1	baking or **western potato**, sliced long way very thinly with a **mandolin**
t.t.	**kosher salt**
t.t.	freshly ground black pepper
	butter to coat pan
2 c.	Tarragon Cream Sauce (recipe follows)

Lightly season the fish with salt and pepper

Butter both sides of each slice of potato. Arrange the slices in an overlapping pattern on a clean working surface.

Place the fish in the center of the potatoes, and carefully wrap a potato slice around each piece of fish. (You may use additional potato slices if needed.)

Using a spatula, transfer the fish to a buttered baking pan and **bake** at 375 degrees until the potatoes are crispy and the fish is flaky—about 12 minutes, depending on the size of the fish.

Serve with Tarragon Cream Sauce.

Tarragon Cream Sauce

3 T.	butter
3 T.	flour
1 pt.	milk, cold
2 t.	fresh tarragon, slightly chopped
t.t.	kosher salt
t.t.	freshly ground black pepper

In a small saucepan over medium heat, melt the butter. Make a **roux** by adding flour and cooking for 5 minutes, stirring frequently.

Add the milk. Bring to a **simmer**, stirring constantly to help prevent lumping.

Add the tarragon, and stir.

Adjust the seasoning with salt and pepper. Add a bit more milk if the sauce is too thick.

Stuffed Sole with Lemon Beurre Blanc

Most of the time sole is stuffed with seafood of some sort. This recipe is different in that it utilizes some fresh vegetables meant to complement the delicate flavor of the fish without overpowering it. The **beurre blanc** is a classic white butter sauce that goes great with lightly flavored fish. If you should prefer a more traditional seafood-bread stuffing, try the Seafood Stuffing recipe on the next page.

This recipe will make 4 portions and take about 30 minutes to prepare.

Ingredients:

4	fillets of sole, any size will do
t.t.	**kosher salt**
t.t.	freshly ground black pepper
	butter, for sautéing and coating pan
1	roasted red pepper, sliced
2 c.	fresh spinach, rinsed
2 c.	**cremini** mushrooms, sliced
	Lemon Beurre Blanc (recipe follows)

Lightly **sauté** the spinach and mushrooms in about a tablespoon of butter, and season with salt and pepper. Reserve.

Lay the fillets of sole, skin side up, on a clean work surface. Dust with salt and pepper.

Divide the vegetables between the fillets of sole, and then place on the fish.

Beginning with the tail end, roll the fish around the vegetable stuffing.

Place the fish in a lightly buttered baking pan so that the seam is down.

Bake at 350 degrees for about 10 minutes or until the fish is flaky and the stuffing is warm.

Top with Lemon Beurre Blanc.

Lemon Beurre Blanc

Ingredients:
1/4 c.   lemon juice
1/2 c.   white wine
2 T.   minced **shallots**
1   bay leaf
5   peppercorns, cracked
1/4 lb.   butter, cubed
t.t.   **kosher salt**

In a saucepan, combine all the ingredients but the butter and salt. Allow to cook over medium heat until reduced by about half.

Strain the sauce to remove the solids.

Remove from the heat and add the butter one chunk at a time, whisking constantly.

When the butter has melted, serve immediately to prevent **breaking** (separation).

Stuffed Shrimp with Seafood Stuffing

These stuffed shrimp are made with a very basic seafood stuffing and taste great. Use whatever size shrimp you like, but remember that the smaller the shrimp, the less stuffing one gets per shrimp. The toughest part of this recipe is taking care not to overcook the shrimp. If overcooked, the texture of shrimp gets downright rubbery.

This recipe will make 4 entrées for most people. For big shrimp lovers, it will serve only 2 or 3. It will take about an hour to make the stuffing, but you can do that ahead of time. Putting together and **baking** the shrimp will take about 15 minutes.

Ingredients:
16   shrimp, 16–20 or larger
       butter to coat pan
       Seafood Stuffing (recipe follows)

If not already done, peel the shrimp and devein deeply along the back. Cutting deep will help the shrimp flare open and hold onto the stuffing.

Form the stuffing into balls that are each about the size of a golf ball.

On a buttered sheet pan, place each piece of shrimp cut side down with the tail up.

Lift the tail out of the way, and place one ball of stuffing on each piece of shrimp. Then fold the tail over the top.

Bake at 375 degrees until the shrimp turn from gray to white, about 8 minutes, depending on the size of the shrimp.

Seafood Stuffing

This recipe is meant to be built upon. It tastes great as is, but you can also use it as the perfect base for the seafood stuffing of your dreams! Try adding 1 cup of **salad shrimp**, imitation or real crabmeat, scallops, or any flaky white fish. Be sure to precook any seafood that you add.

Ingredients:

1/2	loaf bread of your choice, diced
1	red bell pepper, finely diced
1	small onion, finely diced
1	celery stalk, finely diced
1/4 lb.	butter
1 pt.	liquid such as lobster stock, clam juice, or water
2 t.	**Old Bay** seasoning
t.t.	**kosher salt**
t.t.	freshly ground black pepper

Spread the diced bread on a sheet pan, and bake in a 250-degree oven until the bread is dry but not very brown.

In a large pan, **sauté** the pepper, onion, and celery in butter.

When the onions turn **translucent**, add the bread and mix well.

Slowly add liquid until the stuffing reaches the desired consistency.

Add Old Bay, and adjust the seasoning with salt and pepper.

Dijon-Encrusted Salmon

The first time I saw this dish I was doing a restaurant review with my grandmother. She couldn't stop talking about it. It seemed so simple to me that I re-created it and put it on my menu. I'm not exactly sure how the inn we were at made it, but this is what I came up with—and yes, it is grandmother approved.

This recipe will serve 4 and take only 15–20 minutes to make.

Ingredients:

4	salmon fillets, 6–8 oz. ea.
4 T.	Dijon mustard
1 1/2 c.	crushed Ritz-type crackers
3/4 c.	butter, melted, with additional amount to coat pan
t.t.	**kosher salt**
t.t.	freshly ground black pepper

Season the fish with salt and pepper, and place on a buttered pan.

Spoon about 1 T. Dijon mustard over each piece of fish.

In a separate bowl, combine the melted butter and cracker crumbs.

Using your hands, pack the crumb mixture onto the fish.

Bake at 400 degrees until done, about 10 minutes, depending on the size of the fillet.

"The Creator, when he obliges man to eat, invites him to do so by appetite, and rewards him by pleasure."
—Jean-Anthelme Brillat-Savarin

Blackened Salmon with Mango Salsa

I don't really like salmon, but if I had to eat it, this is how I would cook it. Blackening opens up a whole new world of bold flavors that many of us are unaccustomed to. When done well, the char is evident but is balanced with some sweetness and heat. The fresh, colorful mango salsa is a contrast in textures and flavors and also looks great on the plate.

This recipe will serve 4 and take about 30 minutes to make both the fish and salsa.

Ingredients:
4   salmon fillets, 6–8 oz. each
1 c.   Blackening Spice (recipe follows)
2 c.   Mango Salsa (recipe follows)

Dredge the salmon in Blackening Spice until it is well coated.

Place on an extremely hot grill or cast-iron skillet (this will smoke a lot, so I suggest doing it outside on a grill if you don't have an exhaust hood in your kitchen).

Allow the fish to get a dark, rich color on each side, and then remove from the pan or grill. (It will take about 90 seconds per side.)

Finish cooking by **baking** in an oven at 400 degrees or on the grill over indirect heat until done (about 4 minutes).

Top with Mango Salsa, and serve.

Blackening Spice

This is a good basic blackening spice. Feel free to tweak it a bit to your liking, but use only other dry ingredients for a longer shelf life and better blackening.

Ingredients:

6 T.   brown sugar
4 T.   paprika
4 T.   **kosher salt**
2 T.   oregano, dried
1 T.   freshly ground black pepper
2 T.   onion powder
2 T.   garlic powder
1 T.   cayenne pepper (add more or less to taste)

Combine all the ingredients. Wrap tightly and store in a cool, dry place for up to 3 months.

Mango Salsa

This salsa recipe goes awesome with the Blackened Salmon, but you can also use as you would any other salsa. Try it on chips or in tacos, and you'll be surprised at what a bit of mango brings to the party.

Ingredients:

2	mangoes, diced
1	red onion, finely diced
1	red bell pepper, diced
1	large tomato, seeded and diced
1	jalapeno pepper, finely diced (remove membrane and seeds for less heat)
1	lime, juiced
1 T.	cilantro, chopped
t.t.	**kosher salt**
t.t.	freshly ground black pepper

In a mixing bowl, combine all the ingredients.

Season to taste with salt and pepper.

Chef Tip: Why Kosher Salt?

Just about every recipe in this book calls for kosher salt. Most chefs and cooks prefer it for a number of reasons. It's in large flakes, so it's easy to grab a large pinch of it with your fingers. More importantly, though, it doesn't taste as salty as regular finely ground table salt.

Salt should help bring out the flavors of a dish, not make it taste salty. If you don't believe that there's a difference, run a little experiment. Have your own salt tasting by tasting a few granules of different types of salt. Find the one you like best, and use that.

Sesame-Encrusted Tuna Steak with Wasabi Cream

This Asian-inspired dish doesn't mess very much with the great flavor of fresh tuna. The addition of soy sauce adds a touch of salt, and the sesame crust adds a contrasting texture. One doesn't typically think of dairy with Asian foods, but the tartness of the sour cream with a bit of bite from wasabi is a great complement to the tuna. Use the freshest tuna you can find. It doesn't have to be sushi grade, but the flavor and texture are dependent on fresh fish. If you plan on just **searing** the outside of the tuna, freshness is important from a food safety standpoint. Buying tuna that is portioned and flash frozen at sea is a good option.

This recipe will feed 4 and take about 20 minutes to make.

Ingredients:

4	tuna steaks, each 8 oz. and about 1" thick
1 c.	low-sodium soy sauce
1 c.	sesame seeds
1 T.	cracked black pepper
	vegetable oil
1 c.	sour cream
2 T.	**wasabi powder**

Place the tuna and soy sauce in a large self-sealing bag. Remove as much air as you can, and allow to marinate about 15 minutes.

In the meantime, combine the sour cream and wasabi in a small bowl. Set aside.

Combine the sesame seeds and black pepper on a small plate.

Drain the soy sauce from the tuna, and discard the sauce.

Place each piece of fish into the sesame mixture, and press gently to make the seeds stick.

Preheat a sauté pan over medium heat, and coat with oil.

Add the fish to the pan and cook until the crust becomes crispy, about 1 minute per side. This will make fish that is rare to medium rare. If you want it more well done, either turn down the heat to prevent the outside from burning as it cooks or **bake** it in the oven at 400 degrees until it reaches the desired doneness.

Serve with a dollop of the wasabi cream you mixed earlier.

Beer-Battered Fish and Chips

Growing up in New England, I ate lots of fish and chips. Most of the places around here bread the fish with this stuff called **clam fry,** a dry mixture of flours and some seasoning. It's pretty good and what I was used to, but I always thought it was a special treat to go somewhere that served battered fish—crispy golden brown on the outside and soft and doughy around the fish.

This is my take on a basic beer batter. The beer adds carbonation and flavor. Any beer will add carbonation, but use your favorite beer to put your own twist on things.

You'll probably end up with some extra batter, and since your fryer will already be hot, look around the house for other stuff to fry. Veggies like onions and mushrooms work great with this batter too.

This recipe will make 4–6 portions and take about 25 minutes to make.

Ingredients:

5	egg whites
	flour
1 T.	baking powder
1	12-oz. beer
1 T.	**Old Bay** seasoning
1 t.	**kosher salt**
1 t.	freshly ground black pepper
6	fish fillets, about 6 oz. each (cod and haddock work well)
2 c.	flour (as needed)

In a mixing bowl, combine all the batter ingredients, adding only enough flour to achieve a pancake-batter consistency.

Dredge the fish in remaining flour, and then dip into the batter.

Float in 350-degree oil, taking care not to fry your fingers.

Fry until floating and golden brown on the outside.

Serve with tartar sauce, in the Other Cool Stuff section on page 216, French fries, and cold beer.

Lobster Roll

A lobster roll should taste like lobster, be served in a crunchy, buttery warm bun, and be overflowing with lobster salad. New England–style buns are a necessity as they have no crust on the sides of the buns and absorb butter better when grilled. That's all I have to say about that. Here's my take on this New England classic.

These will take about 15 minutes to make, assuming the lobster has already been cleaned. The recipe will yield 4 heaping lobster rolls.

2	lobsters, 1 1/2 lb. each, picked of all meat
4 T.	mayonnaise
3 T.	celery, diced fine
1 t.	lemon juice
1 T.	fresh tarragon, chopped
pnch.	**kosher salt**
pnch.	freshly ground black pepper
4	New England–style hot dog buns
2 T.	butter
t.t.	kosher salt
t.t.	freshly ground black pepper

In a mixing bowl, gently mix together the lobster, mayo, celery, lemon juice, and tarragon. Taste and adjust the seasoning with salt and pepper.

In a sauté pan over medium-high heat, melt the butter and brown both sides of the hot dog buns.

Add the cold lobster salad to the warm rolls, and serve. (Note that some people may enjoy adding a little bit of shredded lettuce to the roll before adding the lobster.)

"If the divine Creator has taken pains to give us delicious and exquisite things to eat, the least we can do is prepare them well and serve them with ceremony."
—Fernand Point

Crab Cakes with Remoulade Sauce

This basic recipe for crab cakes can be made with any type of crab you choose, even imitation crab. There is not as much crab in these as some other recipes, but the combination of ingredients tastes great and is a bit easier on your budget. It's not made with any raw egg, so you can set aside any concerns you may have about tasting before cooking. These work really well dipped in Remoulade Sauce

This recipe will make enough as entrées for 4 people or bite-sized appetizers for 8–10. It will take 30–40 minutes to make.

Ingredients:
1	red bell pepper, diced
1	small onion, diced
1	celery stalk, diced
¼ lb.	butter
½ lb.	crabmeat of your choice (double the amount of crab if you're a crab lover)
3 c.	bread crumbs
3 T.	mayonnaise
2 c.	liquid such as lobster **stock,** clam juice, or water
1 T.	**Old Bay** seasoning
t.t.	**kosher salt**
t.t.	freshly ground black pepper
1 c.	flour
1 c.	Remoulade sauce (recipe follows)

In a large pan, **sauté** the pepper, onion, and celery in butter.

When the onions turn **translucent**, add the crab, mayonnaise, and bread crumbs. Mix well.

Slowly add the liquid until the mixture is moist, but still firm.

Add Old Bay, and adjust the seasoning with salt and pepper.

Form the cakes into the desired size, and **dredge** in flour that's been seasoned with some salt and pepper.

Sauté the crab cakes in vegetable oil over medium-high heat, until warm inside and nicely browned on the exterior. Depending on the size of the crab cakes, this will take 4 to 6 minutes.

Serve with Remoulade sauce.

Remoulade Sauce

This is my twist on the classic French sauce. It strays from the traditional, but the results are great. This sauce works well with most things that you might use tartar sauce on, or break from the norm and try putting it on a burger.

It takes only about 5 minutes to make this sauce. You can easily double or triple it and keep it in the refrigerator for weeks.

Ingredients:

1 c.	mayonnaise
1/4 c.	ketchup
2 T.	yellow mustard
1 c.	relish
1 T.	lemon juice
1 T.	**Old Bay** seasoning
2 t.	kosher salt
2 t.	freshly ground black pepper
2 t.	hot sauce

Combine all the ingredients in a mixing bowl, and mix well.

Chef Tip: Create Extra Counter Space

I've lived in a number of places that had small kitchens with very little counter space. I solved the problem by creating some temporary "counter space" out of tray tables and an ironing board. These worked great, and I could move them into and out of the kitchen as needed. Just be careful not to spill on your ironing board, or it will remind you of what you cooked each time you iron!

Easy Whole Roast Chicken

For years my family and friends have gone to this all-you-can-eat, family-style chicken restaurant in Rhode Island. The chicken tastes great but is sometimes pretty dry, as is much of the chicken served in restaurants. By roasting chicken at home, you can take it out and serve it at just the right time. In this recipe the seasoning is rubbed right onto the bird and flavors the skin, and it also melts during cooking and creates a great sauce for pouring over the chicken as it's served.

One of these chickens will feed 4–6 people as an entrée and take about 1 hour and 20 minutes to make, although only 20 of those minutes is active prep time.

Ingredients:
1/2 lb.	butter
1 1/2 t.	freshly ground black pepper
1 T.	**kosher salt**
1 1/2 T.	onion powder
1 1/2 T.	paprika
1 T.	honey
1	whole chicken, about 3 lb.

Combine all the ingredients except the chicken in a medium saucepan, and bring to a **simmer** to incorporate.

Allow the mixture to cool slightly before rubbing it all over the chicken.

Roast in a small roasting pan at 350 degrees until the chicken is fully cooked, about 1 hour. When it's done the juices will run clear, not pink, and an **instant-read thermometer** placed in the thigh will read an internal temperature of 160 degrees.

Serve with the sauce remaining in the bottom of the pan.

"My doctor told me to stop having intimate dinners for four—unless there are three other people there."
—Orson Welles

Pan-Seared Statler Breast of Chicken with Maple Butter Jus

I learned this recipe while working at a hotel at Dallas-Forth Worth International Airport. It's been my go-to recipe for job interviews or impressing girls ever since. It's relatively easy to make and has a wonderful flavor and texture thanks to the crispy skin. It looks great in a bowl, leaning on a pile of mashed potatoes and surrounded by the sauce. You don't have to use a Statler breast of chicken, which has the first wing segment still attached, but it sure looks cool.

This recipe will yield 4 portions and take you about 20 minutes to make.

Ingredients:
1/4 c.   maple syrup
1/2 c.   butter, at room temperature
4   **Statler** chicken breasts, skin on
2 c.   chicken **stock**
t.t.   **kosher salt**
t.t.   freshly ground black pepper

Mix the butter and maple syrup until combined.

Season the chicken breasts with salt and pepper, and place in very hot sauté pan, skin side down. Cook until the skin turns golden brown.

Turn the breasts over, and cook 2 more minutes.

Turn off the heat, and add the chicken broth to the pan.

Place the pan in a 375-degree oven, and cook until the chicken is done—about 6 minutes, depending on the size of the breasts.

Remove the chicken from the pan, and finish the **jus** by whisking the maple butter into the juices remaining in the pan.

Pour the **jus** over the chicken and serve.

Chef Tip: Brown vs. Black

When cooking, brown is good and black is bad. Any time something you're cooking, or the pan you're cooking it in, turns brown, it means you're developing flavor and color. If the brown stuff is stuck to the pan, you can **deglaze** it with some liquid and use it to flavor your soup or sauce. Use caution, though; there is a fine line between a deep caramel color and flavor and something that is burned. Once things begin to turn black, they get very bitter and can quickly make your entire dish taste burned. Don't be afraid of using hot pans and grills to get color—just be sure you're getting the right color.

Chicken Potpie with Cornbread Crust

Chicken potpie is one of those comfort foods I can't get enough of in the colder months. My perfect potpie consists of big hunks of chicken and vegetables all **stewed** in a thick, flavorful sauce with a touch of cream, all topped with a layer of crusty cornbread. The cream and the cornbread crust really make this recipe stand out when compared to others. This recipe is great to serve family style, or you can make it in individual portions by **baking** in **ramekins** or soup bowls.

This recipe makes 6–8 portions and will take 50–60 minutes to make.

Ingredients:

1 1/2 lb.	chicken thighs (or breast), boneless and skinless, **rough chopped**
2 T.	vegetable oil
1/4 lb.	butter
3/4 c.	carrots, peeled, rough chopped
3/4 c.	onions, peeled, rough chopped
3/4 c.	celery, rough chopped
3/4 c.	flour
1 qt.	chicken **stock**
3/4 c.	peas, frozen
3/4 c.	heavy cream
t.t.	**kosher salt**
t.t.	freshly ground black pepper
1 box	corn muffin mix
	water, as needed

Preheat a **heavy gauge** pot over high heat.

Add the oil and chicken to the pot, and stir until the chicken is brown.

Add the butter, carrots, onions, and celery, and **sweat** them over medium heat until the onions are **translucent**.

Add the flour, and cook 5 minutes to develop a **roux**.

Add the chicken stock and bring the stew to a **simmer,** stirring frequently to prevent scorching.

Simmer 10 minutes.

Stir in the peas and cream, and adjust the taste with salt and pepper.

In a mixing bowl, combine the corn muffin mix with enough water to make the mixture just thicker than pancake batter.

Pour the hot stew into a baking dish.

Pour the corn mixture over the stew so that it's about 1/2" thick.

Place on a sheet pan to make it easier to handle, and **bake** at 350 degrees until the cornbread is cooked and the top is brown, about 20 minutes.

Pancake Chicken with Maple Butter

I invented this recipe totally by accident. I was attempting to bread and **sear** some chicken breasts in hot oil for an upcoming party. Something went wrong with my breading, and it ended up looking like a batter—and tasting like pancake batter! We ended up changing the menu for the party and offering Pancake Chicken with Maple Butter, and it was a hit!

This recipe will make 4 portions and take about 30 minutes to make.

Ingredients:
1 lb.	chicken breast, trimmed of any fat
2 1/2 c.	pancake batter mix, dry
1 1/2 c.	chicken **broth**
t.t.	**kosher salt**
t.t.	freshly ground black pepper
4 oz.	butter, softened, plus some for pan
2 oz.	real maple syrup

Using a meat mallet, pound the chicken breasts until they're about 1/4" thick.

Cut the chicken into desired-sized pieces.

Liberally season the chicken with salt and pepper.

Dredge the chicken in dry pancake batter to coat.

Add the chicken broth to the remaining pancake mix, and stir to incorporate.

In a mixing bowl, combine the butter and maple syrup. Mix well, then set aside.

Dip each breast into the pancake batter, and place in a preheated, buttered sauté pan.

Cook over medium heat until the pancake is golden brown and the chicken is cooked.

Add a spoonful of maple butter to the chicken, and allow to melt into a sauce.

"Eat butter first, and eat it last, and live till a hundred years be past."
—old Dutch proverb

Chicken Mango Curry

I have no training or experience making Thai food, but wow, did this come out great! It utilizes a number of Thai and other Asian ingredients to create a rich, flavorful dish with a taste of heat and sweetness.

Once again, a key to this recipe is to start with a hot pot and **sear** your chicken to develop flavor and color. I prefer to use chicken thighs for their flavor and moisture, but you can use breasts or pretty much any other meat you desire.

This makes for a great meal just served over some jasmine or brown rice. Heck, it's even great over noodles.

This recipe will make 6–8 portions and take about 40 minutes to make.

3 T.	vegetable oil
1 1/2 lb.	chicken thighs, boneless and skinless, sliced into 1" cubes
1	large onion, **rough chopped**
1	green bell pepper, rough chopped
1	red bell pepper, rough chopped
3/4 lb.	sweet potato, peeled, rough chopped
3/4 lb.	**eastern potato**, peeled, rough chopped
1 T.	ginger, fresh, minced
1/4 c.	flour
1	13.5-oz. can coconut milk
1/4 c.	soy sauce
4 T.	curry powder
2 T.	hot sauce
4 T.	honey
1 qt.	chicken **stock**
2	mangoes, peeled, rough chopped (frozen work well too)
1/2 pt.	cherry tomatoes
1/2 c.	fresh basil leaves, removed from stem
t.t.	kosher salt

Preheat a large-bottomed, **heavy gauge** pot over high heat.

Add the oil and chicken, taking care not to get splashed by the hot oil. Sear until the chicken is browned on the outside.

Add the onions, peppers, potatoes, and ginger. Cook until the onions are **translucent**.

Lower the heat to medium low, and add the flour. Cook 5 minutes to create a **roux**.

Add the coconut milk, soy sauce, curry powder, hot sauce, honey, and chicken stock.

Raise the heat to medium high, and bring to a **simmer**.

Add the mangoes, tomatoes, and basil. Simmer 3 or 4 minutes.

Adjust the seasoning with salt and hot sauce, and serve.

General Gau's Chicken

Every Chinese restaurant I go to has a different twist on the General's chicken. I don't really know who the general was, but I hope the recipe I came up with makes him proud. It does me!

If you don't feel like taking out your fryer, you can follow the same recipe but **sauté** the chicken. It's not quite the same, but it's still quite good.

This recipe will serve 4–6 people and take 40–45 minutes to make.

Ingredients:
1 lb.	Boneless, skinless chicken thighs, cut into 1/2" strips
1 c.	soy sauce
2 c.	**cornstarch**
	sliced scallions for garnish
	General Gau's Sauce (recipe follows)

Marinate the chicken in soy sauce at least 30 minutes and up to overnight.

Dredge the chicken in cornstarch until well coated.

Fry at 350 degrees until the chicken is cooked, 5-7 minutes, depending on the size of the chicken pieces. Cut into the largest piece to ensure that there's no pink inside.

Toss the hot chicken with warm sauce, and serve. Garnish with sliced scallions.

General Gau's Sauce

Ingredients:

1 c.	**hoisin sauce**
1/4 c.	soy sauce
2 T.	orange marmalade
1/4 c.	sherry wine
1/4 c.	granulated sugar
2 T.	fresh ginger, chopped fine
1/4 c.	**rice vinegar**
1 T.	fresh garlic, minced

Simmer all the ingredients in a saucepan for 5 minutes.

Orange-Flavored Chicken

This Asian-inspired chicken dish is wicked good. Most of the flavor comes from **simmering** the orange peel in some sugar water, which takes away some of the bitterness of the peel (the peel stays in the sauce) and totally flavors the sauce. You can make the sauce a day or two ahead, but cook and serve the chicken the same day to retain its crispiness.

This recipe will make 4–6 portions and take 40–45 minutes to make.

Ingredients:
1 lb.   boneless, skinless chicken thighs, cut into 1/2" strips
1 c.   soy sauce
2 c.   **cornstarch**
3 T   sliced scallions
         Asian Orange Sauce (recipe follows)

Marinate the chicken in soy sauce at least 30 minutes and up to overnight.

Dredge the chicken in cornstarch until well coated.

Fry at 350 degrees until the chicken is cooked, 5 to 7 minutes depending on the size of the chicken pieces.

Toss the hot chicken with warm sauce, and serve. Garnish with sliced scallions.

Asian Orange Sauce

3	oranges, peeled with vegetable peeler and juiced (save peel)
1 c.	sugar
2 c.	water
1/2 c.	soy sauce
1/4 c.	rice wine vinegar
1/4 c.	**hoisin sauce**
2 c.	chicken **broth**
1/4 c.	honey
1 T.	crushed red pepper flakes
2 T.	ginger, minced
	cornstarch slurry, as needed

Roughly chop orange peel.

Place the chopped peel, orange juice, sugar, and water in a saucepan, and **simmer** 20 minutes.

Add the remaining ingredients except the cornstarch, and simmer 5 minutes.

Using the **slurry,** thicken to the desired consistency.

Honey Sesame Chicken

This dish is prepared using the same method as General Gau's Chicken and Orange-Flavored Chicken. The only difference in the chicken is the addition of sesame seeds. The sauce is sweet and spicy, but the flavor of the honey and the crunch of the sesame seeds really stand out. You can make the sauce up to three days in advance and reheat it for serving.

This recipe will feed 4–6 people and take 40–45 minutes to make.

Ingredients:
1 lb.   boneless, skinless chicken thighs, cut into 1/2" strips
1 c.   soy sauce
2 c.   **cornstarch**
1/4 c.   sesame seeds
          Sesame Chicken Sauce
          sliced scallions for garnish

Marinate the chicken in soy sauce at least 30 minutes and up to overnight.

In a mixing bowl, combine the cornstarch and sesame seeds.

Dredge the chicken in the cornstarch mixture until well coated.

Fry at 350 degrees until the chicken is cooked, 5-7 minutes, depending on the size of the chicken pieces.

Check for doneness by cutting into the largest piece of chicken and looking for pink.

Toss the hot chicken with warm sauce, and serve. Garnish with sliced scallions.

Sesame Chicken Sauce

Ingredients:

1 1/4 c.	honey
1 c.	water
1 1/2 T.	fresh garlic, minced
pnch.	onion powder
1 T.	sesame oil
2 T.	fresh ginger, chopped
2 T.	hot sauce
1/2 T.	hot chili sauce or diced hot peppers
1/2 c.	**rice vinegar**
2 T.	**sweet soy sauce**
	cornstarch slurry, as needed

In a medium saucepan, combine all the ingredients except the cornstarch.

Allow to **simmer** 5 minutes then thicken with the **slurry**.

Satay Chicken Skewers

This Americanized Indonesian dish makes a bright yellow and very flavorful chicken. If you're bored with plain old chicken breasts on the grill, give this dish a try. It involves a quick and easy marinade that you can do ahead of time. Try serving this chicken with the Asian Peanut sauce on page 45.

This recipe will take about 15 minutes to make, not including marinating time. It will produce enough chicken for 4 entrée portions or 8–10 appetizer portions.

Ingredients:

1 1/2 lb.	chicken breast, trimmed of fat and cut into 1/2" strips
1/2	13.5 oz. can coconut milk
1/4 c.	honey
1/4 c.	**rice vinegar**
1/4 c.	soy sauce
2 t.	turmeric
1 t.	hot sauce
	metal or bamboo skewers

Combine all the sauce ingredients in a large self-sealing bag. Seal the bag and shake well.

Add the chicken strips to the marinade, and marinate for at least 30 minutes and up to overnight.

Slide the chicken onto metal skewers or bamboo skewers that have been soaked in water to prevent burning.

Cook over high heat on a grill, over medium-high heat in a sauté pan, or at 350 degrees in an oven for 7 to 9 minutes or until the chicken is cooked.

Serve hot.

"People who are not interested in food always seem rather dry and unloving and don't have a real gusto for life."
—Julia Child

Barbecue Chicken with Peach Barbecue Sauce

This is my favorite barbecue chicken. You can use the basic rub for this chicken on just about anything, or you can even spice up your store-bought barbecue sauce with it. The rub adds lots of flavor to the chicken and will help the sauce better stick to the chicken. The sauce itself isn't too complicated but gets lots of flavor from bourbon and canned peaches.

The recipe calls for whole chicken parts with the skin on, but you can use breasts if you like. Just be careful not to overcook them because they can get very dry.

Another way to tweak this recipe is to bake the chicken with the rub and then put it on the grill with the sauce. This is a great way to make chicken for a crowd because you can cook it the day before and just reheat it and brown the sauce on the grill.

Assuming the sauce is already made, this recipe will take about 30 minutes to make. It will yield enough for 6–8 people.

Ingredients:

1	whole chicken cut into 8 parts
1 c.	Barbecue Chicken Rub (recipe follows)
3 c.	Peach Barbecue Sauce (recipe follows)

Pat the Barbecue Chicken Rub onto the skin of the chicken, and let set for about 10 minutes to allow the rub to soak into the chicken.

Place the chicken on a preheated, medium-high grill, and **grill** 3 or 4 minutes before brushing with the sauce.

Keep brushing with sauce every couple of minutes until the chicken is fully cooked.

Be careful that the sauce doesn't start to burn. If this starts to happen before the chicken is cooked, turn down the heat or move the chicken to a cooler part of the grill.

It will take about 15 minutes for the chicken to cook, depending on the size of the chicken you're using. Use an **instant-read thermometer,** and get the temperature to 165 degrees.

Barbecue Chicken Rub

Ingredients:
1 c.   paprika
1/2 c.   brown sugar
1/2 c.   **kosher salt**
1 T.   onion powder
1 T.   garlic powder
3 T.   freshly ground black pepper
1 t.   cinnamon
1 T.   oregano
1 T.   thyme
1 T.   **liquid smoke**

Combine all the ingredients in a mixing bowl, and mix until combined.

Store in a cool, dry place for up to a month.

Peach Barbecue Sauce

This is a great multiuse barbecue sauce. It's my favorite for pulled pork, but it also works great on chicken and ribs right on the grill. You can also use it as a marinade and for **baking**. The idea of using canned peaches is from a chef I used to work for in Dallas. I love the subtle sweetness they bring to the sauce.
This recipe will make a bit over a half-gallon of sauce. Any extra will keep in the refrigerator for a couple of weeks or in the freezer for up to 3 months. It will take 1 hour and 15 minutes to make the sauce, but it's well worth your time. Try adding a tablespoon of liquid smoke for a smokier flavor.

Ingredients:
1 T.   vegetable oil
1   medium white onion, **rough chopped**
1/2 c.   bourbon or whiskey
64 oz.   Ketchup (any brand will do)

1/4 c.	apple cider vinegar
1 T.	celery seed
1	15-oz. can peaches in syrup, halves or slices
1/2 c.	brown sugar
pnch.	**kosher salt**
pnch.	freshly ground black pepper

Sauté the onion in oil until caramelized.

Add the bourbon, and stir for 1 minute.

Add all the remaining ingredients, and allow to **simmer** at least 30 minutes.

Use an immersion blender to puree.

Adjust seasonings to taste.

If you want a more chunky consistency, finely dice the onion, chop the peaches before adding, and don't puree the sauce.

Meatloaf or Meatballs

Sometimes comfort foods are best untampered with, so you'll find no fancy ingredients or methods here. In fact, I use the exact same recipe for meatballs as I do meatloaf. It's a good-tasting recipe no matter what shape it's in. Often I will form it into a meatloaf and slice it to use in meatball calzones, or I cut it even smaller for meatball pizza. You save yourself from having to spend time getting all the meatballs round.

This recipe will take about 20 minutes to put together. The cooking time depends on what size meatballs or meatloaf you make. You want to reach an internal temperature of 160 and make sure there's no pink inside.

This recipe will make enough meatballs or meatloaf for 8–10 people.

2 T.	butter
1	onion
1/2 c.	Marsala wine
2 lb.	ground beef
3	eggs
1 T.	**kosher salt**
1 t.	freshly ground black pepper
1 t.	garlic powder
2 t.	onion powder
1/4 c.	Worcestershire sauce
2 c.	bread crumbs

Sauté the onions in butter until **translucent**.

Deglaze with wine and allow to cool slightly so that the onions don't cook the meat when you add them together.

Add all the ingredients together, and mix until well incorporated.

Shape or scoop into the desired size, and **bake** at 350 degrees until brown for meatballs and until fully cooked for meatloaf.

"Beef is the soul of cooking."
—Marie-Antoine Careme

American Chop Suey

This recipe comes from one of my grandmother's cookbooks, but I learned it from my mom. This was always a favorite comfort food of mine. There are no secrets revealed in this recipe, but I thought it was worth adding because it's simple and tastes so good!

A few years ago at my buddy Jim's cabin on Lake Wallenpaupack, we made this recipe with some ground venison and it came out great.

Try to mix it with a high-heat rubber scraper (spatula) to help keep the pasta from breaking apart.

This recipe will make enough chop suey for 6–8 large portions and take about 30 minutes to make.

1 lb.	elbow macaroni, cooked
1 lb.	ground beef, 85/15 or however you like it
t.t.	**kosher salt**
t.t.	freshly ground black pepper
2	10 3/4 oz. cans tomato soup concentrate
2 c.	Parmesan cheese, **grated**

In a medium-sized pot, season the beef with salt and pepper and then brown.

Add the tomato soup, and mix well.

Add the pasta and cheese, and mix well using a rubber scraper.

Serve.

"Things should be made as simple as possible, but not any simpler."
—Albert Einstein

Beef Stew

Beef stew is another one of those comfort foods that refreshes and warms your spirit after skiing or shoveling or just working on a cold winter's day. It's pretty darn good in the summer too!

My recipe is relatively basic but uses ketchup and apple juice for more richness and complexity. The key to this dish is to start with a hot pan and allow your meat to brown, developing flavor and color. One other note: don't use expensive cuts of meat. The whole idea of a stew is to take an inexpensive piece of meat and cook it slowly with moisture to make it tender and flavorful.

This recipe will make enough for 8 or so hungry people and take about 40 minutes to make.

1 T.	vegetable oil
1 lb.	lean beef, cubed
1	onion, large, **rough chopped**
2	carrots, large, rough chopped
3	celery stalks, rough chopped
1 lb.	red potatoes, cubed
1/4 lb.	butter
1/4 c.	ketchup
pnch.	dry thyme
1/2 c.	flour
1 1/2 c.	apple juice, cold
32 oz.	beef **stock**, cold
1 T.	Worcestershire sauce
t.t.	**kosher salt**
t.t.	freshly ground black pepper

Preheat a large-bottom, **heavy gauge** pot (at least 8 qt.) over high heat.

Add the vegetable oil, quickly followed by the beef. (Use caution to not splash yourself with hot oil.)

Stir the meat occasionally, allowing it to **sear** on all sides.

Add the onions, carrots, celery, potatoes, butter, ketchup, and thyme. Cook, stirring frequently, until the onions turn **translucent**.

Lower heat to low. Add flour and cook 8 minutes, stirring frequently, to create a **roux**.

Add all the remaining ingredients, increase the heat to medium, and bring to a **simmer**.

Continue to simmer uncovered until the potatoes are tender.

Adjust the flavor with salt and pepper.

For thinner stew, add more stock or water.

Cheeseburger Pizza

This pizza is amazing. It tastes just like a cheeseburger but eats like a pizza. As in the Scallop and Bacon Flatbread recipe on page 27, I use store-bought pizza dough for this recipe. It's too quick and easy to pass up.

Don't get weirded out by the sauce on the pizza, which is ketchup and mayonnaise. Just give it a try. Trust me.

Try to let the dough get to room temperature before working with it, as it will be easier to stretch.

This recipe will take about 35 minutes to make and will feed 4–6 people.

1/2 lb.	ground beef
t.t.	**kosher salt**
t.t.	freshly ground black pepper
1 lb.	pizza or bread dough, room temperature
1/2 c.	ketchup
1/2 c.	mayonnaise
8	American cheese, slices
1	large dill pickle, diced fine
1	tomato, seeded and diced fine
1/2	onion, diced fine

In a medium sauté pan over high heat, brown the beef and season with salt and pepper.

Stretch the dough to the desired size, and place on a baking pan in a preheated 450 degree oven for about 8 minutes to par cook. Remove from the oven.

Spread the ketchup and mayonnaise around to coat the pizza shell.

Cover the entire pizza with 6 slices of American cheese.

Add the beef, pickles, tomatoes, and onions.

Tear up the remaining American cheese and distribute them across the pizza.

Place back in the oven until the cheese browns and the toppings are warm, about 8 minutes.

Serve with shredded lettuce, if desired.

"You better cut the pizza in four pieces, because I'm not hungry enough to eat six."
—Yogi Berra

Country-Fried Steak with Cream Gravy

Country-fried or chicken-fried steak rules. I had to say that. I learned to make this at a hotel I worked at just outside of Dallas, and I've never forgotten it. It's prepared with the same type of breading as fried chicken and then topped with a rich, creamy gravy with sausage. This is another poor man's dish that uses tough cuts of meat but beats them into tenderness. Any piece of well-trimmed beef will work.

For country-fried or chicken-fried chicken, try using chicken instead of beef.

This recipe, including the sauce, will take about 45 minutes to make and will serve as an entrée for 3 or 4 people.

Ingredients:

1 lb.	beef, sliced thinly
3 c.	flour
4 T.	**kosher salt**
2 T.	freshly ground black pepper
2 T.	garlic powder
2 T.	onion powder
4	eggs
2 c.	milk
	vegetable oil for frying
	Cream Gravy (recipe follows)

Place a thinly sliced piece of meat on a clean cutting board, and cover with plastic wrap. Use a meat mallet to pound the beef until about 1/4" thick. Repeat with the remaining meat.

Combine the flour, salt, pepper, garlic powder, and onion powder.

Whisk together the eggs and milk. Set aside.

Dredge the meat into the seasoned flour.

Next, dip the breaded meat into the **egg wash**.

Dredge the meat again in the flour.

Fry at 350 degrees, or **sauté** until golden brown and fully cooked.

Top with Cream Gravy.

Cream Gravy

1	1 lb. log of pork sausage
2 oz.	butter
1 c.	flour
3 c.	heavy cream
3 c.	milk
1 T.	chicken bouillon
2 T.	fresh cracked black pepper

In a wide-bottomed **heavy gauge** pan, brown the sausage over medium-high heat.

Add the butter.

Add the flour, and turn the heat to low. Cook 5 minutes, stirring frequently to make a **roux**.

Add the cream, milk, chicken base, and pepper.

Raise the heat to medium high and bring to a **simmer,** stirring constantly.

If the sauce is too thick, thin with more milk.

Chef Tip: Black Pepper

I prefer black pepper over other types of pepper because I find it less bitter. I also prefer freshly ground black pepper because it has a much stronger flavor. Try some freshly ground black pepper and some preground black pepper, and see whether you can tell a difference. I bet you can!

You can also play with the coarseness of the pepper. For items such as stock, you want the pepper to be whole or in big chunks so that it can be easily strained. Other times you want the big pieces because they add a peppery kick that really comes out when you bite into the food. Still there are times that you want to add a touch of flavor but not any texture or hidden flavors. For these times, use a more finely ground black pepper.

Biscuits and Gravy

You can't beat warm homemade biscuits, and you certainly can't beat them smothered in creamy sausage gravy from page 140. Biscuits and gravy are often served for breakfast, but I think they work well just about any time of day.

The key to making biscuits is in **cutting** in your shortening. You need to get the shortening into small pieces because as it cooks it melts, leaving behind holes in the finished biscuits. The holes are what give biscuits their flaky textures.

This recipe will take about 30 minutes to make, assuming the gravy is already prepared. It will serve 6–8 people.

Ingredients:

5 c.	flour
2 1/2 T.	baking powder
2 1/2 T.	salt
1 c.	shortening
2 3/4 c.	milk, cold
1/2 c.	butter, melted

Combine all the dry ingredients.

Add the shortening, and gently rub between your hands until the mixture resembles oatmeal.

Add the cold milk, and mix just until combined.

Roll out to 1/2" thickness, adding flour if the dough gets sticky, and cut into the desired shape using your knife or a biscuit cutter.

Bake in an oven at 425 degrees for 13 minutes.

Brush with melted butter, and serve or allow to cool for later.

"Don't take a butcher's advice on how to cook meat. If he knew, he'd be a chef."
—Andy Rooney

Salt-and-Pepper Pork Chops

How about some fried pork chops? I have to give credit to a chef I work with, Jim Bird, for introducing me to these at a Chinese restaurant in Boston. The recipe I came up with after eating them is actually pretty simple and tastes so good. I just can't believe it took me so long to fry a pork chop!

This recipe will take about 40 minutes to make, including marinating the pork, and will serve 4–6 people.

Ingredients:

6	pork chops, with or without bone, about 1/2" thick
1 c.	low-sodium soy sauce
1/4 c.	honey
3 c.	cornstarch
6 T.	**kosher salt**
6 T.	freshly ground black pepper
2 T.	garlic powder
2 T.	onion powder
	Vegetable oil for frying

In a large self-sealing bag, combine the soy sauce and honey. Seal and mix well.

Add the pork chops, remove all air, and seal. Allow to **brine** for at least 30 minutes.

Drain the pork, and pat dry with a paper towel.

In a large bowl, combine the cornstarch, salt, pepper, garlic powder, and onion powder.

Dredge the chops in the seasoned flour until well coated.

Fry at 350 degrees until the pork is cooked, about 6 minutes.

Remove the pork from the oil, and drain briefly before serving.

"There is no love sincerer than the love of food."
—George Bernard Shaw

Corn Dogs

Corn dogs are super easy to make at home, and any food you can make on a stick at home is a good thing. We experimented with these for a while at school to try and get them right. We settled on a boxed corn muffin mix and some chopsticks "borrowed" from our favorite Chinese restaurant.

Once we were happy with the breading, we played a bit by using a straw to hollow out some of the dogs. Then we stuffed them with cheese, and cut them into bite-sized pieces before frying. Mmm … good.

This recipe will make 6 corn dogs and will take about 25 minutes to make.

6	hot dogs, whatever brand you prefer
6	pairs of chopsticks, preferably still attached at one end
	cornstarch
1 box	corn muffin mix
1	egg
1/4 c.	milk
2 t.	**kosher salt**

In a large-bottomed pan, combine the corn muffin mix, egg, milk, and salt.

Skewer each hot dog with the loose ends of the chopsticks.

Pour some cornstarch onto a plate, and then roll each dog in the cornstarch.

Dip each dog into the batter, and **float** in a fryer at 350 degrees.

Fry until the batter has set and is golden brown on the outside, about 3 minutes

If the batter is too thick, add more milk.

Starches and Vegetables

Oftentimes people think of starch and vegetable sides that come with our entrées as just "other stuff" on the plate so restaurants don't have to give us any more meat. At some places, that's actually true—but not here in the Land of Wicked Good Food. Each of the following starch and vegetable recipes are good enough to eat on their own as a snack, or dare I say, even as an entrée.

You'll find less than twenty recipes, but they all stand out as either a different twist on a classic or something a bit unusual. I think the potatoes in this section are my favorites. We start with mashed potatoes that consist of three different types of dairy products, and then we move to the best French fries you'll ever have (unless, of course, you were to find some duck fat to fry them in).

These are followed by two types of gnocchi, which are often served as an entrée; my Uncle Cecil's baked beans; and a corn "pudding" recipe that has become a standard at holiday meals at my parents' house.

As you might guess, some of the vegetables are fried, but only a couple. The other vegetables range from incredibly simple, healthy, and tasty grilled asparagus to two Asian-inspired dishes.

I made a point of including only very tasty recipes, so give them a try and you may be surprised that you can actually get people to "finish their vegetables."

"Life expectancy would grow by leaps and bounds if green vegetables smelled as good as bacon."
—Doug Larson

Starch and Vegetable Contents

Mashed Potatoes

It might seem strange to have a recipe for mashed potatoes in a cookbook, but people always compliment the mashed potatoes I make. That's because of my secret ingredient: fat! Don't be shy on the amounts of butter, cream, and sour cream you use. Sure, these potatoes may not be what a doctor would call "heart healthy," but just don't eat the entire bowl. (Once you've tasted these, however, you may find that that's easier said than done!)

This recipe will make enough potatoes for 8 or so people as a side and take 30 minutes to make.

Ingredients:

2 lb.	thin-skinned golden or **eastern** potatoes
1/2 c.	butter, melted (1 stick)
¾ c.	heavy cream
¾ c.	sour cream
1 T.	**kosher salt**
1 t.	freshly ground black pepper

If you don't like potato skins, peel them.

Place the potatoes in enough cold, salted water to cover. **Simmer** until done.

Be careful not to allow the potatoes to sit in water too long after they're cooked, or they'll become wet.

Meanwhile, combine all the other ingredients in a saucepan, and warm. This way the ingredients you add to the potatoes won't cool them down.

In a vessel of your choice, mash the potatoes with the warm cream mixture.

If desired, adjust the seasonings with more salt and pepper.

Chef Tip: Leftover Mashed Potatoes

If you find yourself with leftover mashed potatoes and don't know what to do with them, make soup. Place the potatoes in a pan, and add just enough milk to give them a soup consistency. Adjust your seasonings with some salt and pepper, or take it to the next level by adding a bunch of cheddar cheese, bacon, and scallions to make loaded baked potato soup.

Wicked Good French Fries

Do you want to try the best French fries you've ever had? Make this recipe. It was inspired by the fries I had at my buddy Andy Landry's restaurant in Vermont. There are a few steps to it, but the final result is well worth your effort. Most of the time "homemade" fries are fried twice, once at a low temperature to **blanch** or partially cook them, and then later in hot oil to make them crispy. This recipe uses the same idea, but instead of blanching in hot oil, it uses salted water so that the salt is incorporated right into the potato. They are then dried for a bit in a warm oven, which makes them super crispy when done. Bet you can't eat just one!

Before frying, you can do all of the prep up to a day or two in advance if stored in the refrigerator and up to a month in advance if frozen.

This recipe will make enough fries for 6–8 people as a side or snack and will take about 1 hour to make.

Ingredients:
8   baking or **western potatoes**, cut lengthwise into wedges
1 gal.   water
1/2 c.   **kosher salt** or sea salt
            vegetable oil for frying

In a large sauce pot, combine the water and salt. Add the potatoes.

Allow to cook until the potatoes are **al dente**—soft, but not becoming mushy.

Drain the potatoes, and lay out on sheet pan.

Bake at 250 degrees for about 30 minutes or until the outside of the potatoes are dry.

Deep-fry at 375 degrees until the outside is crispy.

These are also awesome topped with any of the chili or wing sauce recipes found in this book.

Chef Tip: Truffle Ketchup and Malt Vinegar Mayonnaise

For a new twist on two sometimes-boring condiments, try mixing a bit of truffle oil with some ketchup or some malt vinegar with mayonnaise. Look through your cabinets for other things you can add to ketchup or mayo, such as hot sauce, roasted garlic, or curry powder.

Potato Pancakes

These crispy little suckers are well worth the effort of grating a few potatoes. The first time I made them was as an accompaniment to pot roast. After tasting them, I made them several more times just as a snack!

If you choose to make these pancakes extra thick, follow the directions but then finish cooking in a 375 degree oven until the potatoes are tender.

This recipe will make enough pancakes for 6–8 people as a side and take about 30 minutes to make.

Ingredients:

2 lb.	boiling or **eastern** potatoes, peeled
2	onions, minced
1	lemon, juiced
2	eggs
3 T.	flour
t.t.	**kosher salt**
t.t.	freshly ground black pepper
	Vegetable oil, for **sautéing**

Being careful not to grate your knuckles, grate the potatoes.

In a small mixing bowl, toss the potatoes with onions and lemon juice.

Place half the potato mixture on a clean kitchen towel. Fold the towel around the potatoes, and squeeze out whatever liquid you can. Repeat with the remaining potatoes.

In the original mixing bowl, combine all the ingredients except the oil.

Add enough oil to a preheated sauté pan to cover the bottom of the pan.

Spoon about 1/2 c. potato mixture into the pan, and flatten with the back of a spoon. Repeat until the pan is full.

Once the pancakes are browned on one side, flip.

Remove and drain the excess oil on paper towels. Sprinkle with salt.

Potato Gnocchi

These gnocchi are like tiny potato dumplings. You can serve them with any sauce you would typically use for pasta. Their size and soft but chewy texture make them a perfect entrée and not just a side dish to something else. You may skip rolling them off the back of a fork if you like, but this is what makes the gnocchi stand out. Additionally, the little ridges give the sauce a bit more surface area to stick to.

This recipe will take about 30 minutes to make and will serve 6–8 people as a side or 3 or 4 as an entrée.

2 lb.	russet or **western** potatoes, cooked with peels on
2 c.	flour
2	eggs
1/2 t.	**kosher salt**
pnch.	nutmeg
pnch.	freshly ground black pepper

While the potatoes are still hot, run through a food mill (or peel and mash until very fine).

Combine the potatoes with all the other ingredients, and mix only until combined. If the dough is still too sticky, add a bit more flour.

With your hands, form the dough into a rope about 1" in diameter. Cut the rope into pieces about 3/4" thick.

Roll the gnocchi off the back of a fork leaving a small indent in the center. Begin with the cut side because it will stick to the fork better. Cook in **boiling** salted water until the gnocchi float.

Remove from water, toss with your favorite sauce, and serve.

Ricotta Gnocchi

These gnocchi follow the same idea as the potato version but are even easier to make. There are no potatoes to cook, which saves a good amount of time. These are a bit richer than the others because of the addition of cheese and eggs, but they still go well with just about any sauce.

This recipe will make enough for 6–8 people and take about 30 minutes to make.

Ingredients:
15 oz.   ricotta cheese
1 1/2 c. Parmesan cheese, **grated**
3   egg yolks
1/2 c.   chives, chopped
1 T.   **kosher salt**
2 1/4 c. flour

In a mixing bowl, combine all the ingredients to form a firm dough. If the dough is too sticky, add a bit more flour.

With your hands, form the dough into a rope about 1" in diameter. Cut the rope into pieces about 3/4" thick.

Roll the gnocchi off the back of a fork, beginning with the cut side because it will stick to the fork better.

Cook in **boiling** salted water until the gnocchi float.

Remove from water, toss with your favorite sauce and serve.

"When we lose, I eat. When we win, I eat. I also eat when we're rained out."
—Tommy Lasorda

Uncle Cecil's Baked Beans

My great-uncle Cecil was famous for his baked beans. When I got his recipe from my grandmother, it came with a story. Apparently, when preparing beans for church suppers, Uncle Cecil and his wife would make separate batches but use the same recipe … or so she thought. The recipe he wrote down was never quite what he put into his bean pot, thus ensuring that his beans were always better.

I took his "written" recipe and prepared it just as the directions said. I then tweaked some of the amounts just a bit until the resulting beans went from very good to outstanding. I hope these would make Uncle Cecil proud!

This recipe will make enough beans to serve 8–10 people and will take just 15 minutes to put together, but 6 hours to bake.

Ingredients:
2 lb.   navy beans, soaked overnight in 1 gal. water
3/4 t.   baking soda
3/4 lb.   bacon, cut into 1" pieces
2 t.   dry mustard
1 c.   brown sugar
3/4 c.   molasses
1/2 t.   freshly ground black pepper
1 T.   **kosher salt**

In a large pot, bring the beans and baking soda to a **boil**. **Simmer** 5 minutes.

Add all the remaining ingredients, except the salt.

Cover and place in a 350-degree oven for 6 hours.

Add salt and enjoy.

Chef Tip: *Monte au Beurre*
This is a French term meaning "to mount with butter." You can improve just about any soup or sauce by swirling in some room-temperature butter. It adds a bit of viscosity as well as sheen, but more importantly, it adds a rich flavor. Try it in these beans or the next time you make marinara sauce. You'll be amazed at the results.

Corn Pudding

I'm not sure who in my family first found this recipe, but we haven't had a holiday meal without it since it first arrived. It's relatively simple to make and goes great with a traditional Thanksgiving meal or even with barbecue. The result is like a super-moist corn bread that you can eat warm with a fork and knife or serve the next day as just a piece of corn bread.

This recipe will serve 8–10 people as a side dish and will take about 1 hour to make.

Ingredients:

	butter, to coat pan
1	15-oz. can creamed corn
1	15-oz. can whole-kernel corn, drained
1	8.5-oz. box corn muffin mix
1	egg
1 c.	sour cream
1/2 c.	sugar, plus more for dusting

Grease the bottom and sides of a medium sized baking dish with butter.

In a mixing bowl, combine all other ingredients.

Pour into the greased dish, and tap on the counter to make level.

Lightly dust the top with granulated sugar.

Bake at 350 degrees until a toothpick inserted in the center comes out clean.

If you're using a 9" square pan, this will take about 45 minutes.

"Beer is proof that God loves us and wants us to be happy."
—Benjamin Franklin

Rice Pilaf

Rice pilaf is one of those dishes that takes about the same amount of time to make whether you buy a prepackaged mix or do it from scratch. As you will see with this recipe, it's well worth the effort to do it yourself.

Lots of the flavor in this pilaf comes from browning the orzo, so don't be afraid to allow it to get a deep brown. Once simmering, do not stir or the rice will become sticky.

This recipe will feed 6–8 people as a side and take about 30 minutes to make.

Ingredients:
3 T.   oil
1/2 c.   **orzo** , or other interesting small pasta
1 c.   onion, diced
4 c.   chicken **broth**
2 c.   rice
1/2 c.   parsley, chopped

Heat a medium-sized saucepan over high heat.

Add the oil and orzo. Cook until dark brown but not black.

Add the onions and **sauté** 1 minute.

Add the rice and chicken broth.

Mix just to incorporate ingredients.

Bring to a **boil**. Reduce to a simmer, and then cover and cook 20 minutes or until the rice is done.

Stir in the parsley, and serve.

Chef Tip: Cut Onions

There are many old tales of how to prevent yourself from crying when cutting onions, but I haven't found any that actually work and are practical. The best advice I have is to use a sharp knife and to breathe through your mouth. The fumes seem to be less pungent when they don't pass through your nasal passages. If you're really having a tough time and need some relief, stick your head in the freezer and take a couple of breaths. It sounds strange, but it works.

Curried Couscous with Homemade Curry Powder

Couscous is one of those dishes that a lot of people don't think of making at home. I never really understood that because it's so easy to prepare. Simply add boiling liquid, and these tiny bits of pasta cook in just 5 minutes. This particular recipe makes use of a fresh and flavorful homemade curry powder. If you have a favorite store-bought curry, use it to save some time.

This recipe will take about 10 minutes to make and will serve 6–8 people as a side.

Ingredients:

2 c.	**couscous**
1 T.	Curry Powder (recipe follows)
1/2 c.	frozen peas
1/2 c.	red onion, diced very fine
1 t.	honey
1 t.	ground turmeric
2 c.	**boiling** water (or vegetable **stock**)
t.t.	kosher salt
t.t.	freshly ground black pepper

In a mixing bowl, combine all the ingredients except the water or stock.

Add the boiling stock, and wrap the bowl with plastic wrap. Allow to sit for 5 minutes.

Fluff the couscous with a fork, and adjust the seasoning with salt and pepper.

Curry Powder

Homemade curry powder can be a bit time-consuming to make, but boy is it rewarding. Feel free to adjust the ingredient amounts to find your perfect blend. Freshly grinding your own spices makes a big difference in the final taste, but store-bought ground spices can serve as a good substitute. Store in an airtight container, and use as quickly as reasonably possible.

It will take you about 30 minutes to make this recipe.

Ingredients:

1 t.	fennel seed
2 t.	sesame seed
5 T.	coriander
2 T.	cumin
1 T.	turmeric
2 t.	ginger, ground
2 t.	dry mustard
1 1/2 t.	black peppercorns
1 t.	cinnamon
1/2 t.	cloves
1/2 t.	cardamom, ground
1/2 t.	red pepper flakes
1/2 t.	mace
1/2 t.	nutmeg, ground
1 T.	granulated sugar
1 T.	**kosher salt**

In a small dry sauté pan, lightly toast the fennel and sesame seeds over high heat until the pan just begins to smoke. Remove the seeds from the pan so that they stop toasting.

Combine all the ingredients, and crush using a **mortar and pestle** or a home coffee grinder.

Chef Tip: Toast Seeds

Just about any nut or spice that you get whole will benefit from light toasting. This toasting "wakes them up" by releasing stored oils. Toast them in the oven or in a dry sauté pan. Once they begin to jump around or smell nutty, they're done. The longer you cook them, the more of a toasty flavor they'll get.

Coleslaw

I have worked at a number of places that made "homemade" coleslaw by buying precut cabbage and adding dressing out of a gallon jug. This never really made sense to me because of how easily coleslaw can be made and with ingredients most of us already have in our pantry.

Since this recipe's creation, numerous people have asked what brand of dressing we use. I usually offer to give them the recipe—for a price!

This recipe will serve 8 or so people as a side and take about 20 minutes to make.

Ingredients:

1	white cabbage, small
1	carrot, large
1 c.	mayonnaise
1/4 c.	honey
1 T.	celery seed
1/2 c.	cider vinegar
t.t.	**kosher salt**
t.t.	cracked black pepper

Quarter the cabbage, and remove the core. Slice the cabbage as thinly as desired.

Peel and **shred** the carrot.

In a separate large bowl, combine all the other ingredients to make the dressing.

Add the cabbage and carrot to the mayonnaise mixture, and mix well by hand.

Allow to sit 1 hour or more, and then mix again before serving.

Chef Tip: Why Honey Rules

Honey is my favorite sweetener. It has great flavor and is already in a liquid state, so it dissolves and disperses very quickly without heating. Many different varieties of honey are available. All honeys get their flavor not from the bees, but from the flowers that the bees get their nectar from. If the bees are from an orange orchard, for example, the honey will have a subtle orange flavor.

Cucumber Slaw

When I was a kid, one of the snacks I remember my mom making was fresh cucumbers sliced and tossed with a bit of cider vinegar and some sugar. That simple snack, which I still enjoy today, was the inspiration for this slaw. The combination of sweet and sour with the crunch of the cucumbers makes for a perfect side dish on a hot day.

This recipe will feed 6–8 people as a side and take about 15 minutes to make.

Ingredients:

4	cucumbers, peeled, seeded, **julienne**
1	small red onion, sliced very thinly
1 c.	rice wine vinegar
1/2 c.	sugar
3 T.	diced hot cherry peppers (fresh or canned)
pnch.	**kosher salt**

In a small saucepan, combine the vinegar, sugar, peppers, and salt. Bring to a **boil**. Allow to cool slightly.

In a mixing bowl, combine the onion and cucumber. Add the vinegar mixture.

Refrigerate, preferably overnight.

Chef Tip: How to Seed a Cucumber
Without the sometimes-bitter peel and slippery seeds, cucumbers have a great consistent texture and flavor. They are quick to prepare this way and make a big difference in whatever you're making.
Begin by peeling the entire cucumber with a vegetable peeler. Next, cut about 1/4" inch off both ends to remove any flower or stem ends
Slice the cucumber in half lengthwise.
Using a spoon, scrape out the seeds.

Nancy's "Chinese" Coleslaw

As a kid, my family would drive to Indiana to visit relatives at least once every couple of years. They always welcomed us with big smiles and lots of food. The food was never fancy and always flavorful, but it was sometimes a bit odd for a kid from the suburbs.

This recipe is for one of those dishes that I first tried in Indiana and fell in love with. It's an adaptation from my cousin Nancy's recipe. The crunch from the uncooked noodles and nuts make the dish. It's great on its own at a cookout or as a side, especially when paired with Asian entrées.

This recipe will feed about 8–10 people as a side dish and take about 15–20 minutes to make.

Ingredients:

1/2 c.	sugar
1/3 c.	**rice vinegar**
2	seasoning packets from ramen chicken noodle soup
1 c.	vegetable oil
1 lb.	cabbage, shredded
2	carrots, shredded
8	scallions, sliced thinly
1 c.	cashews, lightly chopped
1 c.	sunflower seeds (not in shell)
2	noodles from ramen soup (uncooked)

In a medium mixing bowl, combine the sugar, vinegar, and ramen seasoning. Stir in the oil.

Add the remaining ingredients, except for the noodles. Stir to combine.

Break up the noodles a bit and stir in just before serving.

Broccoli Salad

My mom and I have had many arguments about this summertime family favorite. They all revolve around whether to **blanch** the broccoli. I think that blanching, or partially cooking, the broccoli brightens the color and gets rid of the intense crunch of the raw version. The broccoli still has a good crunch when blanched, but it isn't as dry in your mouth. Try it both ways, but please don't tell my mom if you like her way better.

This recipe will make enough for 8–10 people as a side and will take about 20 minutes to make.

Ingredients:

2 c.	mayonnaise
4 T.	red wine vinegar
3/4 c.	sugar
4	broccoli heads, florets only (a bit over 1 lb.)
8 oz.	extra-sharp cheddar cheese, **shredded**
1 c.	crispy bacon, crumbled
1/2	red onion, finely diced

Blanch the broccoli florets in **boiling** salted water for 1 minute. Remove from the water, and run under cold water to **shock**, or stop the cooking.

In a large mixing bowl, whisk together the mayonnaise, vinegar, and sugar.

Add the broccoli and other remaining ingredients.

Toss the salad together, and serve.

"Vegetables are a must on a diet. I suggest carrot cake, zucchini bread, and pumpkin pie."
—Jim Davis, *Garfield*

Pickled Beets

This dish is basically a recipe for **Harvard beets**, which are typically served warm. My version is relatively sweet with a good vinegar kick. Having a slightly thickened sauce really helps extra flavor stick to the beets. I tend to serve them cold, but serving warm isn't a bad idea either.

This recipe will make enough for 8 or so servings as a side and will take 35 minutes to make.

Ingredients:

1 c.	sugar
2 t.	**cornstarch**
1/2 c.	water
1/4 c.	white vinegar
2	14.5-oz. cans sliced beets, drained
1	onion, sliced thinly

Mix all the ingredients except the beets in a medium saucepan.

Add the beets, turn the heat to medium, and **simmer** 30 minutes.

Allow to cool before serving.

Chef Tip: Let Someone Else Clean Up

If you're doing all the work to prepare a meal, you shouldn't have to clean up. Try and make that arrangement before cooking so you don't run into any arguments.

Now you can say that you read somewhere that the cook doesn't have to clean up, so it must be true!

Applesauce

Applesauce is such a versatile food. It can be eaten hot or cold or as a sauce or snack or side dish, and it makes the whole house smell great while it's cooking. I'm a big fan of going to the orchard in the fall to pick my own apples. The only problem is that I pick way too many. This recipe is a great way to use up those extra apples before they begin to get soft.

Feel free to choose any type of apple for this recipe. Just about any apple will work, but you may have to play with the sweetness or thickness. I personally like to use Cortlands in my applesauce. They have just the right amount of water and sugar, and they break down nicely.

This recipe will make about 8 cups of applesauce and will take you 30 or so minutes to make.

Ingredients:
12	apples, peeled and cored
1 c.	sugar
1/2 t.	cinnamon
1/2 t.	nutmeg
1/2 c.	water
pnch.	**kosher salt**

Combine all the ingredients in a medium saucepan.

Cook over medium heat, stirring occasionally until the apples are soft.

This sauce will be chunky when done. If you want it smoother, run it through a food mill or just stir vigorously with a whisk.

"You cannot sell a blemished apple in the supermarket, but you can sell a tasteless one provided it is shiny, smooth, even, uniform, and bright."
—Elspeth Huxley

Grilled Asparagus

This is probably the simplest recipe in the book, but it's one of my favorites—partly because there are no dirty dishes from preparing it! (Except for a pair of tongs, but you were going to use those anyways.) With the help of a hot grill, you'll have tender, flavorful asparagus in about 2 minutes.

This recipe may be made with as many or as few asparagus spears as you have.

This recipe will serve 4–5 people as a side and will take about 10 minutes to make.

25	asparagus spears, trimmed of any woody ends
	nonstick pan spray
t.t.	**kosher salt**
t.t.	freshly ground black pepper

Place the asparagus spears on a preheated grill so that they're perpendicular to the grill grates, which will keep them from falling through.

Turn the grill off, and spray the asparagus with nonstick pan spray. This is done with the grill off so that the spray doesn't catch fire. (If not using a gas grill, which is easy to light, spray the asparagus while on a plate.)

Turn the grill back on, and sprinkle the asparagus liberally with salt and pepper.

Cook until the tips just begin to brown.

Remove and serve.

"He who eats without drinking dies dry."
—old Roman saying

Beer-Battered Onion Rings

The batter for these onion rings is a basic beer batter that will work well with just about any savory item you can think of. It should come out crispy, puffy, yummy golden brown. I like to use thick slices of onions for a batter like this, as it gives the batter something to stick to.

I like to toss the onion rings in milk before frying, mainly to give the flour something to stick to but also to make the onions a bit less harsh. You can even store them in the milk overnight.

It may seem like you have a lot of batter, but it's much easier to work with too much batter than not enough. If you run out of onions, just find other stuff to fry!

This recipe will make enough onion rings for 8 people as a side or an appetizer. They will take about 30 minutes to make.

Ingredients:

2	onions, ends removed, peeled, sliced into rings at least 1/2" thick
2 c.	milk
1 T.	baking powder
1 T.	**Old Bay** seasoning
1 t.	kosher salt
1 t.	freshly ground black pepper
5	egg whites
1	12-oz. beer of your choice
2 1/2 c.	flour, for batter, as needed
2 c.	flour, for dredging
	vegetable oil, for frying

In a small container, combine the sliced onions and milk. Reserve.

In a mixing bowl, combine the baking soda, Old Bay seasoning, salt, and pepper.

Add the egg whites and beer. Combine.

Slowly add the flour until the batter is the consistency of pancake batter.

Dredge the onions in the 2 c. reserved flour. Lightly shake off any excess flour.

Dip the onions into the batter, and **float** in a 350-degree fryer. Cook until golden brown, about 2 minutes.

Transfer the fried onions onto folded paper towels to drain.

Tempura-Battered Vegetables

Tempura is a light and crispy Japanese-style batter used for frying, most often vegetables. The most important thing about this batter is keeping it cold. This causes a more intense reaction when the food goes into the hot oil, which produces the airy texture. Some vegetables that work well with this batter are broccoli, carrots, onions, peppers, cherry tomatoes, mushrooms, and zucchini and other summer squash.

This recipe will take about 30 minutes to make and will serve 8 or so people as an appetizer or a side.

Ingredients:
4 c.   ice-cold water
4   large eggs
3 1/4 c. flour
8–12   ice cubes
1 T.   **kosher salt**
           flour, for dredging
           vegetable oil, for frying
           vegetables of your choice, peeled and trimmed

Mix all the batter ingredients together (water through salt).

Dredge the vegetables to be fried in the reserved flour.

Dip the food in the batter.

Float into a 350 degree fryer and cook for about 90 seconds or until the food is floating and the outsides are puffy and crispy, but not brown.

"She was so wild that when she made French toast she got her
tongue caught in the toaster."
—Rodney Dangerfield

Desserts

I don't think that a meal is complete without something sweet. My favorite dessert of all time is just a simple cup of homemade ice cream from a little mom-and-pop place. If I couldn't have that, I would choose from one of these dishes.

The recipes I've included run the gamut from a simple, unbaked custard to a traditionally prepared chocolate mousse. You'll even find a newfangled dessert grilled cheese in here. If you want to impress someone, try making the dessert sushi. I promise it has nothing to do with raw fish!

Most of these recipes are things that you've probably heard of or eaten before. I've just added my own little twists and hints. I've also simplified many of the classic methods to make them more efficient for the home cook. That said, these recipes represent how I would make them in a professional kitchen as well.

"Never hesitate to take the last piece of bread or the last cake; there are probably more."
—*Hill's Manual of Social and Business Forms: Etiquette of the Table*
(1880)

Dessert Contents

Key Lime Pie Panna Cotta

I developed this recipe with a former student of mine, Corey Bunnewith, in preparation for a class we were co-teaching. **Panna cotta** is a cooked custard thickened with gelatin instead of the traditional egg yolk. This particular version gets its name from the classic Florida dessert from which it's derived.

This recipe will make 8–10 portions and take about 10 minutes to put together and 1 hour to set.

Ingredients:
1qt.	heavy cream
1/2 c.	granulated sugar
2 T.	honey
2 T.	vanilla extract
1/4 c.	white wine
6 oz.	key lime juice
1 T.	powdered gelatin
1/2 c.	graham crackers, crushed
1	lime, sliced thinly

In a medium sauce pot, whisk together the cream, sugar, honey, and vanilla, and bring to **boil** over medium-high heat.

Reduce the heat, and **simmer** for 3 or 4 minutes

Combine the wine, lime juice, and gelatin in a microwave-proof bowl, and let set until dissolved and thick.

Microwave for 25 seconds to melt the gelatinized mixture.

Add to the cream mixture, whisk, and strain to remove any lumps.

Pour into desired serving dishes, and cool in the refrigerator until firm, about 1 hour, depending on the size of the dishes.

Once firm, garnish with graham crackers and sliced lime.

Dessert Sushi

I got the idea for this dish from a picture I saw in a cookbook when I was in culinary school. It wasn't until years later that I attempted to create it. The recipe is made with a chocolate crepe for the **nori** component, jasmine rice pudding for the rice, and fresh fruit slices as the filling. It took lots of experimentation to make it taste great and look great, but it was well worth the effort. This sushi is something even sushi skeptics will enjoy.

Assuming the crepes and pudding are made, these will take about 20 minutes to make and will serve 4–6 people.

Ingredients:
	Chocolate Crepes (recipe follows)
	Jasmine Rice Pudding (recipe follows)
2	kiwi, peeled and sliced into strips
1	mango, peeled and sliced into strips
4	strawberries, peeled and sliced into strips
	Candied ginger, for garnish

To assemble, lay a 6 × 6 square of crepe on a plastic-wrapped **sushi mat**.

Spread the rice pudding about 1/4" deep across just over half the crepe.

Place the strips of fruit across the length of the rice, about 1" from the edge.

Roll, beginning with the edge closest to you, as you would sushi.

Trim the ends, and cut roll into pieces about 1" thick.

For an added touch, garnish with candied ginger.

Chocolate Crepes

These will take about 30 minutes to make.

Ingredients:

1 1/2 c.	flour
1/2 c.	cocoa powder
6 T.	confectioners' sugar
pnch.	**iodized salt** (iodized is used here because it dissolves better in the batter)
2 T.	vegetable oil
2 c.	milk
2	large eggs
1/2 t.	vanilla extract

Combine all the dry ingredients.

In a separate bowl, combine all the wet ingredients.

Slowly combine the wet and dry ingredients, whisking to dissolve any lumps.

Pour out onto a parchment-lined or greased sheet pan to 1/8" thickness.

Bake at 350 degrees just until firm.

Jasmine Rice Pudding

This will take about 30 minutes to make and another 30 minutes or so to cool.

Ingredients:
3 1/2 c.   cooked jasmine rice
2 c.   milk
2 1/2 c.   heavy cream
2/3 c.   granulated sugar
pnch.   **kosher salt**

Combine all the ingredients in saucepan. Bring to a **simmer** over medium heat, stirring frequently, about 20 minutes or until a spoon will almost stand alone.

Refrigerate until cool.

Chef Tip: Carry a Knife

It may seem obvious to many, but there is a proper way to walk with a knife. Always carry it with the tip pointed down and the knife next to you. Also, never use your knife to point at things. This way if you drop it or get bumped or startled, you'll, hopefully, avoid impaling anyone, including yourself.

Cannoli Bites

These little hors d'oeuvres are everything cannoli have but in easy-to-eat, one-bite forms. They're much easier to make than homemade cannoli and taste just as good. Instead of forming the shell, you shape them into whatever shape you want and then fry. Spoon a dollop of filling on top, and you're done. The only issue is that this version makes it much easier to lose track of how many you've eaten!

This recipe will take about 30 minutes to make and will serve 8 people.

Shell "crackers" ingredients:
1 1/2 c.	flour
1 T.	granulated sugar
pnch.	**iodized salt**
1/2 c.	Marsala wine
2	egg whites, beaten

Topping ingredients:
2 c.	good quality ricotta cheese (not too watery)
1 t.	citrus **zest** (lemon, lime, or orange)
1/2 c.	heavy cream
3/4 c.	confectioners' sugar
2 T.	liqueur (optional)

Combine the flour, sugar, and salt. Add the wine, and mix until a stiff dough forms. Allow to rest 1 hour.

Roll dough out to about 1/8" thickness, and cut into desired shapes.

Fry at 350 degrees until golden brown and crispy. Drain on paper towels.

If you desire, you can also **bake** these at 350 degrees for about ten minutes, but the texture will not be as good.

For the topping, combine all ingredients in a mixing bowl.

To assemble, spoon or pipe the filling onto the cannoli shell "crackers" and serve.

"Leave the gun. Take the cannolis."
—Clemenza, in *The Godfather*

Chocolate Rum Truffles

I created this recipe with the help of one of my students who wanted to make something different to add to her desserts. We got lots of compliments using these rich, melty, chocolaty balls just as garnishes on other desserts. They also make the perfect dessert **hors d'oeuvre** or can help you get over the end of your most recent relationship. It may even be worth breaking up with someone just so you have an excuse to eat a bunch of these!

This recipe will take about 30 minutes to make and 2 more hours to firm up in the refrigerator. Depending on the size of the truffles, this recipe will make about 25.

Ingredients:
10 oz.   semi-sweet chocolate, chopped
6 T.   butter
1 c.   heavy cream
2 T.   corn syrup
1/2 c.   rum of your choice
         cocoa powder, for coating

In a small saucepan over medium-low heat, melt the butter then remove from the heat. Add the chocolate, and melt.

Add the remaining ingredients, and mix to incorporate.

Pour into a small baking pan, and refrigerate until cool and firm (about 2 hours).

Scoop into desired-size balls.

Roll in cocoa powder.

Serve from the refrigerator for more firm truffles, or leave out for about 1 hour before serving for a softer texture.

"A good cook is like a sorceress who dispenses happiness."
—Elsa Schiaparelli

Lemon Granita

Lemon Granita, a frozen ice with the tang of lemon, is a fantastic thing to have in the freezer on a hot summer day. This is a basic recipe that you can build off of. Play around with different flavorings by removing the juice of one lemon and adding some espresso or rum extract. For a lemon lime granita, use only one lemon and add the juice of two limes.

This recipe will serve about 8 people and take about 1 hour to make.

Ingredients:
8 c.   water
2 c.   sugar
2   lemons, juiced

Boil 2 c. water. Add the sugar, and stir until dissolved.

Pour the syrup and any flavorings into the remaining water.

Pour in a baking pan, and place in the freezer so that the pan is level.

Freeze, stirring every 10 minutes or so, until the dish is completely frozen but has an airy, granular texture.

Press plastic wrap directly on the frozen granita, and keep in the freezer until needed.

Chocolate Mousse

This mousse recipe is certainly more complicated than adding cream to a boxed mix, but I'm guessing it will be the best mousse you've ever had. *Mousse* literally translates to "froth" or "foam" in French, and that's exactly what you're making. You create the body of your mousse by whipping air into egg whites and cream.

Take your time when folding your mousse together. Your goal is to pop very few of the air bubbles that you took the time to make.

This recipe calls for eggs which do not get cooked. There is actually little danger in using raw eggs as long as you always use very fresh eggs that have been properly refrigerated. If you are apprehensive about using raw eggs, purchase pasteurized egg whites and yolks at your local supermarket.

This recipe will take about 30 minutes to make and will yield enough for 8–10 desserts, depending on the size.

Ingredients:
1 lb.	semisweet chocolate
8 oz.	heavy cream
8	egg yolks
4 oz.	granulated sugar
8	egg whites
2 oz.	granulated sugar
8 oz.	heavy cream

Melt the chocolate and cream together over a double boiler or in a metal bowl placed atop a smaller pan filled with simmering water. Reserve this chocolate mix.

Whip the yolks and sugar by hand until light and fluffy, about 1 minute. Reserve.

Using an electric mixer, whip the whites and sugar into firm peaks. Reserve.

Use the mixer to whip the cream into soft peaks. Reserve.

Now that all the mixing is done, it is time to combine all these different elements.

Fold the chocolate mix into the yolks.

Fold the chocolate and yolks into the whites.

Fold the egg mix into the cream.

Serve chilled.

Gingerbread Whoopie Pie

Mmm … whoopie pies. This childhood favorite takes on new life when you use gingerbread as the cake. These delicious little treats are surprisingly simply to make and come out so good. Play around by adding your favorite flavorings or liqueurs to the filling, or soak the cakes with some cinnamon schnapps to make them a bit more adult.

This recipe will take about 45 minutes to prepare and will make 8 or so whoopie pies.

Ingredients:

1 c.	vegetable oil
1 c.	granulated sugar
1 c.	molasses
2	eggs, lightly beaten
3 c.	flour
1 T.	ground ginger
2 t.	cinnamon
1 t.	**iodized salt**
1/4 t.	cloves
1 c.	water
1 T.	baking soda

Filling ingredients:

½ lb.	butter
½ c.	all-purpose vegetable shortening
1 c.	**confectioners' sugar**
2 c.	marshmallow creme, such as Fluff
1 t.	vanilla extract

In a mixing bowl, add the oil, sugar, molasses, ginger, and eggs. Whisk to incorporate.

Add the flour, ginger, cinnamon, salt, and cloves. Mix until combined.

In a small saucepan, **boil** water. Add baking soda, and then whisk into the batter.

Using a 4-oz. ladle or a 1/2 c. measuring cup, ladle the batter into separate piles on a sheet pan covered with **parchment paper**. **Bake** at 350 degrees for 14 minutes or until set. Allow to cool before filling.

To make the filling, place all the ingredients in the bowl of a mixer. Mix on high until very smooth, about 5 minutes.

Once the cakes are cool, assemble by spooning about 1/2 c. filling onto half of the cakes. Cover with the remaining cakes.

Easy Crème Brulee

Traditionally, crème brulee is made in a few steps. You have to **simmer** the vanilla bean with the cream, then separate the eggs and whisk the yolks with the sugar, and then **temper** the yolks into the warm cream.

This recipe skips those steps to make it easier for the home cook, yet still produces a crème brulee that is pretty darn close to the classic. The most important step in this recipe is to allow your sugar to dissolve, or it will settle on the bottom of your crème brulee while **baking**.

This recipe will take about 10 minutes to put together and another hour or so to cook. It will make 6–8 portions.

Ingredients:
1 qt.   heavy cream
1 t.   vanilla extract
1 c.   granulated sugar
6   egg yolks
6 T.   granulated sugar,

Combine all the ingredients, except 6 T. sugar, in a mixing bowl.

Whisk until the sugar is dissolved.

Divide into 6 **ramekins** (6–8 oz. each).

Bake in a **water bath** at 325 degrees until set, about 45 minutes to 1 hour.

Allow to cool.

Spoon 1 T. of sugar onto each custard, and brown the sugar using a blowtorch or your broiler.

Serve immediately.

"Try not to use your smoke alarm as a timer."
—Matt Williams

Pumpkin Crème Brulee

This recipe follows a more traditional procedure than the previous Easy Crème Brulee. With many of the same seasonings as pumpkin pie, but richer and with a much creamier texture, this recipe makes the perfect dessert for a fall evening.

This recipe will take about 1 hour to make and will serve 6 people.

Ingredients:

1 1/2 c.	heavy cream
1/2 c.	milk
6	egg yolks
1/2 c.	canned pumpkin
1/2 c.	granulated sugar
1/2 t.	vanilla extract
pnch.	cinnamon, ground
pnch.	nutmeg, ground
pnch.	ginger
	butter, as needed
4 T.	granulated sugar

Whisk together all the ingredients, except 4 T. of sugar, in a mixing bowl until the sugar is dissolved.

Butter 6 **ramekins,** and pour the mixture into each.

Bake in a **water bath** for 40 minutes or until the mixture firms.

Place in the refrigerator until thoroughly cool.

Divide the remaining sugar, and sprinkle on top of each custard.

Brown the sugar using a blowtorch or broiler.

Churros

When made at home and served fresh, these little Mexican doughnuts can't be beat. They're so much better than their dried-out, fast-food counterparts. Crispy on the outside and a bit doughy in the center, these churros provide a great contrast in textures. Try dipping them in chocolate sauce for an extra treat.

This recipe will take about 30 minutes to make and will make enough churros for 8–10 people.

Ingredients:
1 c.	sugar
1 t.	ground cinnamon
4 c.	water
1 lb.	butter
1 T.	**iodized salt**
4 c.	flour
12	eggs, beaten together

In small bowl, combine sugar and cinnamon.

Heat the water, butter, and salt to a rolling **boil** in a large saucepan.

Add the flour and stir vigorously over low heat until the mixture forms a ball, about 1 minute. Remove from the heat.

Add the eggs to the pan, and stir until incorporated.

Spoon the mixture into a **pastry bag** fitted with a large **star tip**.

Pipe onto the flat part of a spatula, and slide into a 350-degree fryer. Fry until golden brown, turning once.

Dip in the cinnamon sugar mixture, and serve.

Pineapple Upside-Down Cake

I'm not a huge fan of most cakes. The traditional layer cake with frosting certainly has its place and can be done very well, but give me a piece of pineapple upside-down cake any day. You can make an upside-down cake with just about any fruit, but pineapple is the most popular. The wonderfully sweet and fruity topping is actually created in the bottom of the cake pan and is flipped over only after the cake is **baked**.

This recipe will take about 2 hours to make and will feed 12 people.

Topping ingredients:

12 T.	butter
1 1/2 c.	brown sugar
3 T.	rum (preferably dark)
2 lb.	pineapple (rings look nice)
	maraschino cherries, as needed

Cake ingredients:

3 c.	flour
2 1/2 t.	baking powder
1/2 t.	cinnamon
1/4 t.	nutmeg
1/2 t.	**iodized salt** (table salt)
1 1/2 lb.	butter, room temperature
2 1/2 c.	granulated sugar
6	eggs
1 c.	milk

For the topping, combine the butter, rum, and sugar in a medium saucepan. Bring to a **simmer**. Reserve.

Start the cake by sifting together all the dry ingredients except the sugar.

In a mixer, **cream** together the butter and sugar. Add the eggs one at a time.

Alternate adding the milk with the flour mixture until incorporated.

Prepare large baking dish by greasing with butter. Cut **parchment paper** the size of the bottom of the pan, and lay in pan. Grease the paper as well.

Place the pineapples and cherries in the bottom of the pan.

Pour the topping mixture over the fruit.

Pour the batter over the topping so that it coats it evenly.

Bake, with a cookie sheet below to catch any drips, at 350 degrees until a toothpick inserted in the middle comes out clean, about 1 hour 30 minutes.

Cinnamon Rolls

Okay, so these take some time to make, but they make the whole house smell so good. This recipe purposely makes more cinnamon rolls than you can eat in a day. Why? Because if you're anything like me, you *will* eat quite a few warm ones before sharing them.

This recipe will take about 3 hours to make and will yield about 1 dozen large cinnamon rolls.

Dough ingredients:

4	eggs
4 oz.	granulated sugar
6 oz.	butter, melted
1 1/2 c.	buttermilk (milk may be substituted)
4 1/2 c.	flour
1 1/2 T.	active dry yeast
2 t.	**kosher salt**

Filling ingredients:

4 c.	brown sugar
4 T.	ground cinnamon
4 oz.	butter, melted

Icing ingredients:

3/4 c.	cream cheese
1/2 c.	milk
4 c.	powdered sugar

In the bowl of a mixer, combine all the ingredients except the flour. Whisk together.

Add the flour, and mix with a dough hook on low speed for 10 minutes.

The dough should be soft and moist but not sticky. If sticky, add a bit more flour.

Form into a ball, cover with a damp rag, and place in a warm place until doubled in size (about 1 hour 30 minutes).

While dough is rising, combine all icing ingredients using a mixer with a whip attachment, and mix all filling ingredients in small mixing bowl just to combine.

Punch down the dough, and divide in half.

Roll each piece of dough into a rectangle about 12" × 32".

Spread the filling equally onto each piece of dough, leaving about 1" along the top edge with no filling.

Brush the top edge with **egg wash,** and carefully roll the dough so that you finish with the egg-washed seam on the bottom.

Cut each log into 1 1/2" pieces.

Place the pieces about 1" apart in a buttered baking dish, and let rise about 30 minutes.

Bake at 325 degrees for about 25 minutes or until the internal temperature reaches 190 degrees.

Drizzle the rolls with icing, and serve warm.

Red Velvet Cake

This cake was my grandmother Dorchester's specialty. Every Christmas Eve, I looked forward to having this cake at my grandparents' party. She typically made it only once a year, except for a couple of birthdays when I must have been a particularly good those years.

The cake is a chocolate cake that uses some vinegar to help with rising and red food coloring for its characteristic color. The cake is very good on its own, but the frosting is what makes it. Unlike any frosting I've ever made, it's actually cooked and then mixed with **creamed** butter and sugar. It's awesome!

This recipe will take about 1 hour 30 minutes to make and will yield 1 tall 9" cake. That's enough for at least a dozen people.

Ingredients:

2 1/2 c.	flour
1 1/2 c.	granulated sugar
1 t.	baking soda
1 t.	**iodized salt** (table salt)
1 t.	cocoa powder
1 1/2 c.	vegetable oil
1 c.	buttermilk, at room temperature
2	eggs, at room temperature
2 T.	red food coloring (1 oz.)
1 t.	distilled white vinegar
1 t.	vanilla extract
	Frosting (recipe follows)
2 c.	pecan pieces for garnish (optional)

Preheat the oven to 350 degrees. Lightly oil and flour 3 (9" × 1 1/2" round) cake pans.

In a large bowl, sift together the dry ingredients.

In another large bowl, whisk together the wet ingredients.

Using a mixer, mix the dry and wet ingredients until just combined and a smooth batter is formed.

Divide the cake batter evenly among the prepared cake pans.

Bake until the cake pulls away from the sides of the pans and a toothpick inserted in the center comes out clean—about 30 minutes.

Remove the cakes from the oven, and run a knife around the edges to loosen them from the sides of the pans.

One at a time, invert the cakes onto plates and then re-invert them onto a cooling rack, rounded-sides up. Let cool completely.
Using a long, serrated knife, even off the tops of the cakes.

Frost the tops of each layer, and then assemble into one cake.

Frost the sides and any other spots that need it.

It's very important to keep this cake refrigerated.

Sprinkle the top with pecans, if desired.

Red Velvet Frosting

5 T.	flour
1 c.	cold milk
1 t.	vanilla
1 c.	granulated sugar
1/2 lb.	butter

In a small saucepan, mix together the milk and flour. Slowly bring to a **simmer** and cook 5 minutes, stirring often to prevent burning. The mixture will get very thick.

In a mixing bowl with a whip attachment, mix the sugar, vanilla, and butter on medium speed for 15 minutes. (Yes, 15 minutes.)

Add the flour mixture to the butter mixture, and mix until smooth.

Chef Tip: Hot Pans

Anytime you take something out of the oven or walk away from a hot pan, flag it. This involves simply hanging a kitchen towel or hot pad over the edge or handle of the pan to let others know that it's hot. This is especially important during holidays when there are many cooks in the kitchen.

Chocolate Doughnut Bread Pudding with Hard Sauce

Wow, this is good! I once worked at a conference center that threw away dozens of doughnuts every day. I thought that was kind of wasteful, so I invented a way to use them and my cholesterol hasn't been the same since! This is a pretty basic bread pudding recipe except that it replaces bread with doughnuts. Use any kind of doughnut you like, except for ones with crème fillings.

The **hard sauce** is called that because it becomes hard when refrigerated but melts when served on this warm pudding.

This recipe will make enough bread pudding for 8–10 portions in about 40 minutes.

Ingredients:

3	doughnuts, chocolate cake, glazed
3	doughnuts, glazed
6	eggs
2 c.	heavy cream
2 t.	vanilla
pnch.	nutmeg
1/2 c.	granulated sugar
2 oz.	butter
	Hard Sauce (recipe follows)

Grease a medium size baking pan with butter.

Cut or tear doughnuts into hunks about 1" in size. Add to the greased pan.

In a mixing bowl, mix the eggs, cream, vanilla, nutmeg, and sugar until incorporated. Pour over the doughnuts. Mix to ensure that all the doughnuts are covered in the custard mixture.

Bake at 350 for 20–25 minutes or until the pudding reaches an internal temperature of 165 degrees.

Serve warm, with hard sauce, or cold. Allow to cool slightly before slicing.

Hard Sauce

1/2 lb.   butter
2 c.   **confectioners' sugar**
1 t.   vanilla extract
3 T.   whiskey

Cream the butter and sugar in a mixer until smooth. Add the vanilla and Whiskey, and mix until incorporated.

Refrigerate.

Deep-Dish Apple Pancake

The inspiration for this came from a big pancake I had at a local pancake place. When I decided to try and re-create it, this is what I came up with. It works just fine as a breakfast item, but I like it even more as a dessert. It has some sweetness—although not overly sweet—and has the consistency of a dense custard. It's pretty unique. I hope you like it. For some variety, try making it with other types of fruit, such as bananas or pears or a combination of fruits.

This recipe will take about 1 hour to make and will yield 6 or so portions.

Ingredients:

1 ½ c.	flour
1 t.	**iodized salt**
1 c.	**confectioners' sugar**
3/4 t.	baking soda
1 1/2 t.	baking powder
3 c.	heavy cream
4	eggs
2 oz.	butter, melted
1 t.	vanilla
4	apples, peeled, cored, and diced
cinnamon, as needed	

Mix the dry ingredients together in a large mixing bowl.

Add the wet ingredients. Mix until just combined.

Place the peeled fruit in a greased baking dish, about 10" × 12" in size. Sprinkle with cinnamon.

Pour the batter over the fruit. **Bake** at 350 degrees about 45 minutes or until done.

"I went to a restaurant that serves 'breakfast at any time.'
So I ordered French toast during the Renaissance."
—Steven Wright

Apple Crisp

I always wanted to eat at my grandmother Williams's house just in case she made her apple crisp. I'm not sure what exactly went into her topping, but I think it may have just been butter and sugar with a sprinkle of flour. This recipes uses some oats for a bit more texture, but it isn't missing any of the flavor. If you like cinnamon, sprinkle some on the apples before covering with the topping.

This recipe will make enough for 6–8 portions and take a little under 1 hour to make.

Ingredients:
3/4 lb.	butter, softened
1 1/2 c.	brown sugar
3 c.	oatmeal
1 1/2 c.	flour
1 T.	vanilla
6	baking apples of your choice (Cortlands work well), peeled and sliced

Combine all the ingredients using a mixer with a paddle attachment. Mix until well combined.

Place the apples in a 10" square baking dish.

Crumble the topping onto the sliced apples.

Bake at 400 degrees until the apples are soft and the crust has begun to brown—about 35 minutes.

"Do or do not. There is no try."
—Yoda

Peach Cobbler

Peach cobbler is one of those southern comfort foods that every cook should have in his or her repertoire. Once you have a basic cobbler recipe, you can substitute just about any canned or fresh, ripe fruit.

This recipe is relatively simple—just make sure not to stir everything together in the baking dish. Things are purposely poured in layers because the batter will rise and go all around the peaches, and the butter will rise to the top and then soak back into the dough as it bakes.

This recipe will make about 12 servings and take about 1 hour to make.

Ingredients:

1/4 lb.	butter, melted
1 1/2 c.	granulated sugar
1 1/2 c.	flour
3/4 T.	baking powder
1/2 t.	**iodized salt** (table salt)
2 c.	whole milk
2	29 oz. cans peaches in syrup, drained

Pour the melted butter into a preheated medium size baking dish.

In a medium mixing bowl, combine the flour, sugar, baking powder, and salt.

Slowly add the milk to the dry ingredients to create a batter.

Pour the batter over the pan of melted butter. Do not mix.

Distribute the peaches over the batter. Do not mix.

Bake at 350 degrees for 45 minutes or until a toothpick stuck into the center comes out clean.

Indian Pudding

An old-fashioned dessert that originated in New England, this is basically a baked cornmeal pudding that's flavored with molasses and spices. It takes some time to make but is pretty easy to put together. The only challenge is not sneaking a taste before it's done **baking**.

This recipe will take about 2 hours to make and will yield 6–8 portions.

Ingredients:

2 c.	milk
1/2 c.	cornmeal
1/4 c.	granulated sugar
1/4 c.	brown sugar
1/2 c.	molasses
1 t.	iodized salt
3 T.	butter
1/4 t.	cloves, ground
1/2 t.	ginger, ground
1 c.	milk
2 c.	heavy cream

In a medium saucepan, combine the milk and cornmeal. Bring to a **boil**, and then cook over medium heat, stirring constantly, until the mixture is as thick as oatmeal.

Add all the remaining ingredients.

Transfer to an oven-safe pan, and bake in a **water bath** for 1 hour 30 minutes, stirring every 30 minutes.

Serve with a spoonful of hard sauce from the Chocolate Doughnut Bread Pudding recipe on page 200, or top with ice cream.

Molten Chocolate Cake

This dish is one of the coolest desserts ever. It's a really rich chocolate cake batter that is purposely undercooked, served hot, and, if done correctly, will be filled with warm, gooey chocolate. Top with a bit of fresh whipped cream and some berries, and I promise you won't be disappointed.

Before you make this for guests, prepare a test version to figure out the ideal cooking time for your oven and baking dishes.

This recipe will take about 30 minutes to make and will serve 8 or so portions, depending on the size muffin tin you use.

Ingredients:
11 oz.   butter
10 oz.   semisweet chocolate, chopped
6   eggs
6   egg yolks
3 c.   **confectioners' sugar**
1 c.   flour

In a small saucepan, melt the butter and then remove from heat. Add the chocolate, and stir until melted.

In the bowl of a mixer, mix the eggs, yolks, and sugar. Whip until smooth.

Add the chocolate mixture to the egg mixture. Mix until incorporated

Add the flour, and mix until just incorporated.

Pour the batter into well-greased muffin tins of desired size.

Bake at 450 degrees until the outside is set and the inside is very runny, about 4–6 minutes.

Serve immediately.

Dessert Grilled Cheese with Mascarpone and Caramelized Bananas

Wow, these are good! I was trying to come up with a new bite-sized dessert for a class I was teaching and happened to read something about a grilled cheese. That was my inspiration for making a dessert grilled cheese. These are great served at a party in bite-sized pieces or eaten whole while sitting on your couch.

This recipe will make about 20 appetizer-size portions and will take about 20 minutes to make.

Ingredients:
10	slices of bread of your choosing (sourdough works well)
8 oz.	mascarpone cheese
2 T.	**confectioners' sugar**
2	ripe bananas, sliced
1 T.	granulated sugar
4 oz.	butter, melted

Remove the crust from the bread, and cut into bite-sized pieces that are the shape of your choice. Discard the crust or save for breadcrumbs or croutons.

In a small mixing bowl, combine the cheese and powdered sugar.

In a sauté pan over medium heat, lightly caramelize the bananas with the granulated sugar and about 1 oz. of butter. Reserve.

Build the grilled cheeses by placing a heaping teaspoon of cheese and one slice of banana on half the pieces of bread. Top with the remaining pieces of bread.

Brush the bread with melted butter, and place in a sauté pan over medium heat.

Cook, turning once, until the bread is golden brown and beginning to crisp on both sides.

Allow to cool for a couple of minutes before attempting to cut.

"A dinner which ends without cheese is like a beautiful
woman with only one eye."
—Jean-Anthelme Brillat-Savarin

Cake Doughnuts

Cake doughnuts are quicker and easier to make than their yeast-raised counterparts, but they certainly aren't lacking in quality. It's a matter of personal preference as to which type you like best. I actually like my yeast doughnuts filled or frosted, while I prefer cake doughnuts for mixing flavorings into the dough itself. Feel free to play around and add items such as fruit and nuts to spice things up a little.

This recipe will take about 1 hour to make and will yield enough doughnuts for 6–8 people.

2	eggs
1 c.	granulated sugar
1 c.	milk
4 T.	shortening, melted
4 c.	flour
4 T.	baking powder
pnch.	cinnamon, ground
pnch.	nutmeg, ground
pnch.	**iodized salt** (table salt)
1 c.	**confectioners' sugar,** for glaze
3/4 c.	cool water

In the bowl of a mixer, combine the egg, sugar, and shortening using a paddle.

Add the remaining ingredients, and mix until smooth.

Allow to rest in the refrigerator for 30 minutes.

On a lightly floured surface, roll the dough to about 1/2" thickness.

Cut into desired shapes, and fry at 350 degrees until lightly brown on both sides and not doughy in the center.

Make a glaze of confectioners' sugar mixed with about 3/4 c. water. Add more water for thinner glaze.

Dip the doughnuts into the glaze, and serve.

Yeast Doughnuts

The great thing about making doughnuts at home is that they can become whatever you want them to be. They can be any size, shape, color, or flavor. This recipe is great all by itself, but it takes on a whole new life when you dip the doughnuts in chocolate, glaze with royal icing, fill with your favorite jam or jelly, or simply sprinkle with sugar. Use your imagination, and you will be amazed at what you can come up with.

This recipe will take about 2 hours to make and will yield enough doughnuts for 10 or so people.

1/4 c.	butter
2/3 c.	**scalded** milk
2/3 c.	warm water (110 degrees)
1 1/2 oz.	active dry yeast
3/4 c.	granulated sugar
5 c.	flour, sifted
2	eggs, lightly beaten
1 t.	**iodized salt** (table salt)
1 t.	cardamom, ground
1/2 t.	cinnamon, ground
	vegetable oil, to coat dough

Combine the butter and milk.

In a medium mixing bowl, mix the water, yeast, and sugar. Add the milk mixture and eggs. Mix to combine.

Add the remaining ingredients, and mix until smooth.

Lightly coat the dough with oil, and place in a warm place to rise until doubled in size, about 1 hour.

Punch down the dough, and roll out to approximately 1/2" thickness. Cut to the desired shape.

Allow to rise 20 minutes.

Deep-fry at 360 degrees until golden brown and fully cooked in the center.

Other Cool Stuff

This last section of recipes has a number of things that I wanted to show you but that didn't really fit into the other categories. Some of them are pantry items that you can make ahead and have on hand if the need arises, while others are pretty random.

Most of these recipes are sauces that are cheap and easy to make at home, such as tartar sauce, salsa, and chocolate sauce. Others recipes include things you may not have considered making at home, such as taco seasoning, granola, and hot chocolate mix.

Flip through the pages, and see whether you already have the ingredients to make any of these items. Give them a try!

"The only real stumbling block is fear of failure. In cooking you've got to have a what-the-hell attitude."
—Julia Child

Other Cool Stuff Contents

Salsa

This simple salsa recipe is a great way to utilize garden-fresh tomatoes in the summer. If local ripe fresh tomatoes are not available, it is fine to use good quality whole canned tomatoes that you can dice to your desired size. Feel free to add just about any other vegetable to it for added flavor and texture. As you'll see below, I like to puree the salsa and add some chunks back to it, but if you like it super chunky and without much sauce, skip the blender all together.

This recipe will make about 4 cups of salsa and should take about 20 minutes to make.

Ingredients:

2	large tomatoes, seeded and diced
1	onion, large, diced fine
2	bell peppers (the more colorful the better), diced fine
2	limes, juiced
1/2 c.	corn kernels, fresh or frozen
1 T.	honey
1 t.	**kosher salt**
2 t.	hot sauce
1/4 c.	cilantro, chopped

Combine all the ingredients in a mixing bowl.

Remove 1 cup of salsa, and puree in a blender.

Add the puree back to the salsa, and mix to combine.

"Si squid deest, addes.
If something is missing, add it."
—Apicius

Tartar Sauce

Homemade tartar sauce can't be beat, especially because most of us have all of the ingredients for it already hanging around our kitchen. In its simplest form, tartar sauce is just mayonnaise mixed with sweet pickle relish. This recipe adds a touch of acid from some lemon juice, and some Old Bay seasoning for a different twist.

This recipe will yield about 5 cups of tartar sauce and take about 5 minutes to make.

3 c.	mayonnaise
2 c.	sweet relish
3 T.	lemon juice
1 T.	**Old Bay** seasoning

Combine all the ingredients in a mixing bowl.

Store in the refrigerator in a tightly sealed container for up to 2 months.

"One cannot think well, love well, sleep well, if one has not dined well."
—Virginia Woolf

Cranberry Sauce

You can make this easy homemade cranberry sauce with either fresh or frozen cranberries. The acid and sweetness from the oranges and a touch of thyme really make this sauce stand out. For a smooth sauce without skins, strain before chilling.

This recipe makes about 6 cups of sauce and will take about 20 minutes to make.

Ingredients:

6 c.	cranberries, fresh or frozen
2	oranges, **zest** and juice
3/4 c.	water
1 1/2 c.	sugar
1/2 t.	cinnamon, **grated**
1/2 t.	thyme
2 t.	**cornstarch**

Combine all the ingredients in a medium saucepan, and bring to a **boil**. Lower the heat, and **simmer** for 5 minutes. Serve either warm or cold.

Marinara Sauce

This quick marinara sauce gets a great burst of flavor from fresh basil leaves and garlic. It doesn't cook very long, which allows the garlic to retain some of its bite. The sauce works great on pasta and pizzas or even as a dip.

This recipe will make a little over 1 quart of sauce and take 25 minutes to make.

Ingredients:

1/2 c.	extra virgin olive oil
1	onion, **rough chopped**
2 cl.	garlic, peeled with dry ends removed
2	28-oz. cans whole peeled pear tomatoes
1 t.	**kosher salt**
1/2 t.	freshly ground black pepper
1 c.	fresh basil leaves

In a large **heavy gauge** pan over medium-high heat, sweat the onion and garlic **cloves** in oil for 5 minutes.

Add all the remaining ingredients.

Puree using an immersion blender.

Bring to a **simmer,** and allow to cook 10 minutes.

Chef Tip: Olive Oil Differences

Buying olive oil can be confusing because of all the different possible names on a label. The best is extra virgin olive oil from the first cold pressing (using no heat or chemicals) because it has the lowest acidity, fruitiest flavor, and greenest color. Virgin oil is also good but has a slightly higher acidity. Light olive oil is light in flavor and color, not calories. This is due to a very fine filtering process.

Like fine wines, olive oils will vary in flavor depending on where the olives were grown. Test different varieties until you find one you love. Also try to use a bottle of oil in a few months, as all oils will develop off flavors over time.

Parmesan Crisps

These crunchy little critters have only one ingredient: Parmesan cheese. This recipe is essentially melted cheese that becomes very crispy once cool. You can even form the cheese into shapes. They go great on a Caesar salad or as a cool garnish standing in a pile of mashed potatoes.

This recipe will take about 15 minutes to make and will yield enough cheese crisps for 4–6 people.

Ingredients:
2 c.   Parmesan cheese, **shredded**

Preheat your oven to 350 degrees.

Scoop out 2 T. cheese at a time, and make piles about 2" apart on a sheet pan.

Using your fingers, spread the cheese out a bit so that it isn't piled higher than 1/4".

Bake until the cheese has melted and is beginning to brown around the edges.

Once out of the oven, either allow to cool or immediately form into shapes.

To form into shapes, remove from the pan with a spatula and mold into a small cup or over a rolling pin. Or just cut or fold into the shape you want. Be sure to work quickly, though, as the cheese will begin to set as soon as it starts to cool.

"One can never know too much; the more one learns, the more one sees the need to learn more and that study as well as broadening the mind of the craftsman provides an easy way of perfecting yourself in the practice of your art."
—Auguste Escoffier

Taco Seasoning

This taco seasoning is better than anything you can buy in the store, and it's made with ingredients most people have hanging around in their cupboard. Even if you have to go out and buy something, you'll make your money back with your first batch of seasoning. You can make a larger batch and store it for a couple of months in a tightly sealed jar. Use this recipe as a starting point to create your own signature blend by playing with amounts or adding other ingredients.

This recipe will take about 10 minutes to put together and will make just over 2 cups of seasoning.

Ingredients:
1 c.   paprika
1/4 c.   onion powder
1/4 c.   garlic powder
1/4 c.   cumin
1/8 c.   oregano
1/4 c.   kosher salt
4 T.   brown sugar
1/8 c.   freshly ground black pepper

Combine all the ingredients.

Store in a cool, dry place for up to 2 months.

Chef Tip: SPGO (Salt, Pepper, Garlic, Onion)

I always have a mixture of kosher salt, black pepper, garlic powder, and onion powder around the kitchen. It's a great basic seasoning for just about any savory dish. I typically use one part each of pepper, garlic powder, and onion powder and two or three parts salt. This saves me having to open or even search for these things separately while cooking.

Granola

This very basic recipe uses ingredients most of us already have in our kitchen. The oatmeal gives it body, and the water, which almost entirely **evaporates**, holds it all together. Everything else adds different flavors and textures. Feel free to add whatever you want until you come up with your favorite recipe.

This will keep in a cool, dry place for up to a month, but I guarantee it won't last that long!

This recipe will make about 10 cups of granola and will take about 1 hour to prepare.

Ingredients:

4 c.	oatmeal
1 c.	pecan pieces
1 c.	almonds, sliced
1/2 c.	poppy seeds
1 c.	cornmeal
2 c.	brown sugar
2 t.	kosher salt
1 c.	water
1 1/2 c.	raisins

On a large sheet pan, combine all the ingredients, except the raisins, and mix well.

Bake in a 275-degree oven for 45 minutes. If you have a **convection** oven, be sure that the fan is on.

Stir occasionally to allow the granola to dry evenly.

Once cool, add the raisins.

Store in a cool, dry place.

Hot Chocolate Mix

One day a student asked me whether I'd ever made my own hot chocolate mix. I had never even thought of such a thing. He was interested in trying it, so we did some research and experimentation and came up with this recipe. It contains similar ingredients to store-bought mixes but with a bit of spice from some cayenne pepper. Don't be afraid to play with the proportions a bit to suit your tastes.

This recipe will take about 5 minutes to make and will yield about 30 portions, depending how chocolaty you like it.

Ingredients:

2 1/4 c.   **confectioners' sugar**
1 c.   cocoa powder
2 1/2 c.   powdered milk
1 t.   **iodized salt** (table salt)
2 t.   **cornstarch**
1/4 t.   cayenne pepper

In a medium mixing bowl, combine all the ingredients.

Stir into a cup filled with hot water, just as you would store-bought hot chocolate mix.

Chef Tip: Have a Can-Do Attitude

Don't be afraid of anything in the kitchen. If you see or read about or taste something you'd like to make at home, go ahead and try it. It may not come out exactly how you want, but you will definitely learn something from the process and will be closer to doing what you'd hoped.

Cashew Brittle

Brittle is called brittle because it's brittle. Say that three times quickly. Brittle is just melted sugar with something—in this case, cashews—mixed in. Once it's cool, it breaks into chunks relatively easily, thus giving brittle its name. You can add almost anything to brittle, as long as it won't melt. Nuts are the favorite, but seeds and dried herbs and spices can be fun too. I've even given some interesting brittles out as Christmas gifts.

Just remember that caramelized sugar is wicked hot, so be careful not to get it on you.

This recipe will make a cookie sheet full of brittle and will take you about 30 minutes to prepare.

Ingredients:
2 c.   granulated sugar
1/2 c.   water
1 c.   cashews

In a clean sauce pot, combine the sugar and water.

Cover and **simmer** over high heat for 3 minutes.

Remove the lid, and cook until the bubbles get large and the sugar begins to caramelize.

Spread the nuts out over a cookie sheet.

Pour the sugar onto the cookie sheet, covering the nuts. Ensure that the pan is on a surface that won't burn, as the sugar will be extremely hot.

Allow to cool before breaking into chunks.

Coffee Syrup

Coffee syrup and all things made with coffee syrup are Rhode Island specialties. I first heard of the syrup, used in all the same ways one would use chocolate syrup, from some friends of the family who always had this mysterious ingredient at their home. I'd look forward to going there just so I could have some ice cream loaded with coffee syrup.

Coffee syrup still isn't readily available outside of Rhode Island, so I decided to try to make my own. I came up with this and haven't bought coffee syrup since. It's great in milk or over ice cream, and it adds a little flair to sweet or even savory dishes.

This recipe takes about 15 minutes to make and yields 2–3 cups of syrup.

Ingredients:
2 c.   coffee
1 1/4 c. granulated sugar
1/2 t.   vanilla
1   shot of espresso

Combine all the ingredients, and allow to **simmer** for 5 minutes. Store for up to a month sealed in the refrigerator.

"Part of the secret of success in life is to eat what you like and let the food fight it out inside."
—Mark Twain

Chocolate Sauce

This is the quickest, easiest chocolate sauce recipe that I know of. It's also super tasty. There are only three ingredients, all of which are pretty good on their own: chocolate, butter, and heavy cream. This recipe doesn't use a double boiler, which many recipes call for when melting chocolate. This is because we melt the butter first and only have the chocolate over the heat briefly. The rest of the melting happens from **residual heat**.

This recipe will take about 15 minutes to make and will produce about 5 cups of sauce.

Ingredients:
1/4 lb. butter
3 c.   semisweet chocolate, chopped or morsels
2 c.   heavy cream

In a small saucepan over medium heat, melt the butter.

Add the chocolate, and stir constantly for 1 minute.

Remove from heat, and continue to stir until the chocolate is completely melted. (You may return the pan to the heat if needed, but do it briefly and always keep stirring.)

Stir in the cream.

Store in the refrigerator up to 2 weeks. The sauce will get very thick when cold, so warm it up in a warm **water bath** or in brief increments in the microwave.

Crème Anglaise

Crème Anglaise translates literally to "English cream." It's a rich, custard-based sauce that is typically served cold but can also be served warm. It's also very similar to the base for vanilla ice cream. It is a great tasting sauce that can be used on or around just about any dessert.

Don't tell anyone, but there have been occasions where I've simply melted some good-quality ice cream to make a reasonable substitute for this sauce. It tastes great but isn't quite as thick.

This recipe will take about 20 minutes to make and will yield about 6 cups of sauce.

Ingredients:
4 1/2 c. heavy cream
2 t.   vanilla extract
12   egg yolk
1 c.   granulated sugar

In a medium saucepan, combine the cream and vanilla. Bring to a **simmer,** and then shut off the heat.

While the cream is heating, whisk together the yolks and sugar.

Temper 1 c. of cream mixture into the egg mixture.

Pour the egg mixture back into the pot, stirring constantly.

Sauce should **nappe,** or stick to the back of a spoon. If it doesn't, gently heat until it reaches the desired consistently.

Be careful to not allow the eggs to scramble.

Afterword

I hope that after reading this book and making some of these recipes, you've become a better cook. Whether you're a first-timer or a seasoned veteran of the kitchen, I hope I've made you think about food a bit and enjoy what can sometimes be a chore. I also hope that I've been able to inspire you to cook outside your comfort zone and play with your food using the freshest local seasonal ingredients you can.

Lastly, I hope that you will give copies of this book to all your families and friends and pretty much anybody else you know.

"Now you know, and knowing is half the battle!"
—G.I. Joe

About the Author

Matt Williams was born and raised in Marlborough, Massachusetts. His first cooking experiences came when making boxed macaroni and cheese with his brother and fighting over who could put the cheese in. He later cooked for church and Boy Scout fund-raisers and even spent a summer working in a hot dog truck.

His first taste of professional cooking came at age sixteen when he was told to get a job and wound up working for a chef friend of his dad's at a local conference center. Making, and eating, thousands of mozzarella sticks and turning whipped cream into butter helped to light his passion for food.

After high school, Matt attended Johnson and Wales University in Providence, Rhode Island. While there he earned both an associate's degree and a bachelor's degree in culinary arts and a master's degree in education with a concentration in foodservice. He has worked and taught all over the country, including Nantucket, Massachusetts; St. Petersburg Beach, Florida; Dallas, Texas; Atlanta, Georgia during the 1996 Summer Olympics; San Jose, California; Vail, Colorado; and Washington DC.

He is currently the lead instructor of the culinary arts department at Blackstone Valley Regional Vocational Technical High School in Upton, Massachusetts. In 2007 he began the Sweet Potatoes Cooking School, which specializes in custom-designed cooking classes in the comfort of your own home.

Matt and his wife, Jane, currently live in central Massachusetts where they are both public school teachers and recently welcomed into their family a daughter named Lucy. They spend much of their summer vacations together on Cape Cod and the rest of their time eating around and exploring New England and wherever else life takes them.

Appendix A
Table of Weight and
Measurement Equivalents

1 teaspoon	1/3 tablespoon
3 teaspoons	1 tablespoon
1/2 tablespoons	1 1/2 teaspoons
2 tablespoons	1 ounce; 1/8 cup
4 tablespoons	2 fluid ounces; 1/4 cup
5 1/3 tablespoons	1/3 cup
8 tablespoons	4 fluid ounces; 1/2 cup
12 tablespoons	6 fluid ounces; 3/4 cup
16 tablespoons	8 fluid ounces; 1 cup; 1/2 pint
1 cup	8 fluid ounces
1/2 cup	4 fluid ounces
1/4 cup	2 fluid ounces
1 pint	2 cups; 16 fluid ounces
1 quart	4 cups; 2 pints; 32 fluid ounces
1/2 gallon	8 cups; 4 pints; 2 quarts; 64 fluid ounces
1 gallon	16 cups; 8 pints; 4 quarts; 128 fluid ounces

Appendix B
Table of Metric Equivalents

I've rounded these equivalents up or down a bit to make measuring easier. I haven't listed all the possibilities, as I assume you or someone you know has some basic math skills and can convert these measurements further.

1/4 ounces	7 grams
1/2 ounces	15 grams
1 ounce	30 grams
8 ounce (1/2 pound)	225 grams
16 ounces (1 pound)	450 grams
2 1/4 pounds	1 kilogram
3 pounds	1.4 kilograms
4 pounds	1.8 kilograms
1/4 teaspoon	1.2 milliliters
1/2 teaspoon	2.5 milliliters
1 t teaspoon	5 milliliters
1/2 tablespoon	7.5 milliliters
1 tablespoon	15 milliliters
1/4 cup	60 milliliters
1/3 cup	75 milliliters
1/2 cup	125 milliliters
3/4 cup	175 milliliters
1 cup	250 milliliters
2 cups (1 pint)	500 milliliters
1 quart	1 liter

Appendix C
Recipe Conversion

Recipe conversion is great in that you can make a recipe for six people serve two or sixteen or even sixty people. You first have to figure out a conversion factor. Next you multiply the ingredient amounts from your recipe by this number. This will give you the amount needed for the new number of portions.

This applies to most ingredients in most recipes, but you need to use a bit of common sense as well. If you double or triple a recipe, for example, there's a good chance you'll need a larger pan or more time, or both. You may also need to cook things in batches, especially fried items. In this case, you don't need to double or triple the amount of oil, just the amount of times you use it.

Follow these steps to figure out the conversion factor:

Determine how many portions your current recipe makes.
Determine how many portions you need.
Divide the portions you need by the portions the recipe currently makes.
The answer to this is the conversion factor.
needed / currently makes = conversion factor

Multiply the ingredients in the recipe by the conversion factor to determine the new amounts.

Appendix D
Listing of Chef Tips

Glossary

A

Adobo sauce: A dark red paste made from ground chilies with vinegar. Canned **chipotle** peppers are usually packed in adobo sauce.

Al dente: An Italian phrase that means "to the tooth." It is used to describe the degree of doneness of some foods, especially pasta. The cooked food should offer a bit of resistance when bitten and not be soft or mushy.

Aromatic: Plants, herbs, and spices that have pungent aromas and add strong flavors to food. They're typically used as seasonings, not the main item.

B

Baking: A **cooking method** in which food is in an enclosed space and is surrounded by dry heat, such as an oven.

Beurre blanc: A French sauce meaning "white butter." This is made from a seasoned white wine **reduction** to which chunks of room-temperature butter are added while the sauce is constantly stirred. The butter adds richness as well as sheen and texture to the sauce.

Bisque: A thick, creamy soup in which all the ingredients are pureed.

Blanch: A method by which a food is partially cooked to brighten its color or to reduce cooking time later. Once removed from the heat, the food is usually **shocked** in cold water to stop the cooking process.

Boiling: A **cooking method** where food is plunged into 212-degree, intensely bubbling water. This method is too damaging for many foods, which are better prepared by **simmering** or **poaching**.

Boursin: A smooth, white cheese with a high fat content, often sold seasoned with garlic and herbs.

Braise: A combination **cooking method** where a large piece of meat is **seared** on the outside with a dry cooking method, then **simmered** in liquid until tender.

Breaking, sauce: When the fat separates from the rest of a sauce, leaving a greasy puddle on top of a liquid that often gets a bit chunky. This can be caused by overheating a sauce or by adding too much fat to a sauce.

Brine: A solution of water and salt, often with a type of sugar, used to add moisture and flavor to food. Poultry and pork benefit greatly from brining.

Broiling: A dry heat **cooking method** where the food is placed below the heat source and allowed to cook from the top.

Broth: The result of **simmering** meat, fish, or vegetables in water. Used for flavoring soups and sauces.

Brown butter: Butter that has been allowed to cook until the sugars in it begin to caramelize and the fat begins to brown. It has a pleasant, nutty aroma and taste.

C

Calibrate: To determine the accuracy of a thermometer or other measuring device.

Chipotle pepper: A dried and smoked jalapeno pepper. Often sold canned and packed in **adobo** sauce. Chipotles can also be found dried or pickled.

Clam fry: A fine flour used for breading seafood. It's primarily composed of corn flour with cornmeal to give it a yellow color and has some baking powder that acts as a **leavener**.

Clarified, butter: Butter that has been simmered slowly until it separates into three layers. Any solids are skimmed off the top and the bottom layer, a milky liquid, is removed. This leaves a clear butter which has a higher smoke point, or burning temperature.

Clove, garlic: One individual segment of a bulb or head of garlic.

Confectioners' sugar: Also called 10X sugar or powdered sugar, this finely ground granulated sugar is bright white in color and has a small amount of **cornstarch** added to prevent clumping.

Convection movement: The movement of heat around a product. The heat may be transferred through hot air, hot oil, or hot water. This movement promotes even cooking and reduces cooking times.

Cooking methods: The foundation of cooking. All heat transfer happens through one cooking method or a combination of cooking methods. Using the appropriate cooking method for a particular food will greatly influence its taste, texture, and color.

Cornstarch: A powdery white thickening agent made from the endosperm of corn kernels. It thickens instantly when heated, so it's typically mixed with a cold liquid and poured into whatever needs to be thickened. Unlike flour-based thickeners, items thickened with cornstarch will be clear and not opaque.

Couscous: Typically tiny Moroccan pasta made of **semolina** flour. Couscous does not need to be **boiled** like other pasta. Pouring the proper amount of boiling liquid over it and covering for five minutes results in fully cooked couscous.

Cream: The process of combining two or more ingredients until a soft, smooth texture is achieved. In baked goods, this is most commonly done with sugar and a fat, such as butter or shortening. Once creamed, the mixture should not separate or be granular at all.

Crème Anglaise: A rich custard-based sauce often served with desserts.

Cremini: A baby portabella mushroom. It is brown in color and is slightly more firm than a button mushroom.

Crostini: Translated from Italian to mean "little toasts," crostini are small, thin, toasted pieces of bread. They are typically brushed with olive oil or butter and allowed to cook slowly so that they get crispy all the way through.

Cutting: The process of combining a cold, solid fat with dry ingredients until a mealy texture is formed, with small bits of fat completely covered in dry ingredients. This mixing method is essential to biscuits, as the melting of the bits of fat leave air pockets that make the biscuits flaky.

D

Deep-frying: A **cooking method** where food is completely submerged in hot fat. The food is often coated with some sort of breading or batter to protect or contain the item and to add crunch.

Deglazing: The process of adding a liquid to a hot pan in order to remove any caramelized bits of food left on the bottom of a pan after **sautéing**. The resulting flavorful liquid is often used to create a sauce for the sautéed dish.

Dredge: To dip a piece of food into a flour or bread crumb mixture to lightly coat it before frying or **sautéing**. The food is usually damp, which helps the breading to stick.

E

Eastern potatoes: Also known as boiling potatoes or waxy potatoes, these are lower in starch and higher in sugar than **western potatoes**. This makes them more suitable for **boiling** than **baking**. New potatoes, young potatoes of any variety, have similar characteristics and can be used for similar dishes.

Egg wash: A mixture of egg yolk or whole eggs mixed with water or milk. Egg wash is brushed on baked goods to add color and shine and is used to help breadings stick when frying.

En papillote: Cooking food inside a pouch made of **parchment paper**. The pouch is sealed to trap steam from the food, which aids in cooking. Dishes served en papillote are typically served still in the paper for the eater to cut into.

Evaporation: The process of a heated liquid releasing steam and water vapor. This causes the amount of liquid in the pan to **reduce** as steam goes into the atmosphere.

F

Float: To slowly and carefully place food into hot oil while still holding the other end of the food. This is done to prevent items from sticking to each other or from sinking to the bottom and becoming stuck on the basket. The food is dipped in and allowed to fry briefly before letting go.

Folding: The process of carefully combining two items, at least one of which is light and airy, while trying to break as few air bubbles as possible in order to maintain volume. Folding is done by pulling a rubber spatula through and around the items to be combined and actually folding it onto itself until the desired mixture is achieved.

G

Gemelli: A shape of pasta made by twisting two short tubes of noodle together.

Grating: The process of reducing the size of an object into an almost powdery consistency. Grating is often done to hard cheeses such as Parmesan. A box grater or food processor is a good tool for this job.

Grilling: A **cooking method** where food is placed on a grate above a heat source and allowed to cook. The heat source radiates waves of heat that cook the rest of the food. The hot grates of the grill transfer heat directly, causing browning and flavor development on the food.

H

Hard sauce: Made by beating butter, sugar, and sometimes flavorings together until smooth. It is solid when cool, and then softens and melts when placed on warm food.

Harvard beets: Usually served hot as a side dish, these sliced beets have been **simmered** in a thickened sauce and flavored with vinegar and sugar.

Heavy gauge: Refers to the thickness of metal in a pot or pan. With thicker metal there is more even heat distribution, and the pan's ability to hold onto heat increases when cold food is placed into it.

Heel: The portion of a knife blade that extends from the beginning of the handle to the cutting edge. When choosing chef or French knives, the heel should be long enough to prevent your fingers from touching the cutting board while cutting.

Hoisin sauce: A sweet and spicy Chinese barbecue sauce made primarily of soy beans and flavored with garlic, chili peppers, and spices.

Hone: The process of straightening the cutting edge of a knife. Even a sharp blade will need to be honed because the fine cutting edge will bend through normal use. Honing is not meant to sharpen a knife, only to help maintain the cutting edge.

I

Instant-read thermometer: A small thermometer used for taking the temperature of meat and baked goods toward the end of cooking. It typically has a 1" dial and a 5" probe. The probe end is inserted into the food so that the tip is in the center of the item. This will give the most accurate internal temperature and will read the temperature in a matter of seconds.

Iodized salt: Common table salt that is ground with the addition of iodine, which can be an important dietary supplement. It is ground to a fine grain and has additives to assist in free flow.

J

Julienne: A matchstick-shaped knife cut of a vegetable. It measures 1/8" × 1/8" × 2".

Jus: A French term for natural juices created from cooking meat. A dish served with these juices is referred to as "au jus."

K

Kosher salt: A coarse-grained or flaky salt that is free of additives. It gets its name from its use in making meat kosher. Kosher salt is preferred because it lacks the metallic taste often associated with **iodized salt**.

L

Leaveners: Used in many baked goods to increase volume by making a batter or dough rise. Baking soda, baking powder, and yeast are all leaveners that will release carbon dioxide gas, create bubbles in an uncooked dough or batter, and increase size while lightening texture. Items such as angel food cake are leavened by beating air into the batter to create the same type of bubbles.

Liquid smoke: A flavoring dissolved from the resin left behind from smoking foods or made directly from the burning of hardwood wood chips or sawdust. It adds a distinct smoked flavor without the trouble of smoking something at home. Liquid smoke is very potent and should be added a few drops at a time.

Lo mein: A Chinese dish made of cooked noodles **sautéed** or stir-fried, typically in a **wok**, with meats and vegetables and often seasoned with a soy sauce–based sauce.

M

Mandolin: A hand-operated tool used for uniform cutting and slicing of firm vegetables and fruits. Often has adjustable or interchangeable blades to create a variety of shapes and different-sized cuts.

Masa harina: Translated from Spanish as "dough flour," it's the ground corn flour used for making corn tortillas. It's also a great addition to southwestern or Mexican food as a thickener.

Mise en place: A French term meaning "everything in its place" and the cornerstone of successful cooking. It refers to doing all of your prep work, including fully reading and understanding a recipe, cutting and measuring all ingredients, and having all necessary equipment ready before beginning to cook.

Mortar and pestle: The mortar is a bowl and the pestle is a cylindrical object with a rounded end made to fit comfortably in one's hand. They are usually made of the same material. The pestle is pressed against the interior of the mortar to grind food items to the desired consistency.

N

Nappe: A term used to describe the thickness of a sauce. A sauce at this thickness will evenly coat the back of a spoon with a thin layer without immediately dripping off.

Nori: Very thin sheets of dried seaweed, often used for rolling sushi.

O

Old Bay: A seafood seasoning developed and used heavily in the Chesapeake Bay region on crabs and shrimp. It's a blend of spices, including celery salt, pepper, bay leaves, ginger, and cinnamon. Although traditionally a seafood seasoning, it may be used on just about anything.

Orzo: Tiny rice-shaped pasta.

P

Panna cotta: Translated from Italian as "cooked cream," it's thickened custard made without eggs. Because it's thickened with gelatin, panna cotta is always served cool.

Parchment paper: Thick paper treated with silicone to be nonstick and resistant to moisture and grease. It can be used to **bake** on, wrap things **en papillote**, or even make bags for piping ingredients such as frosting or chocolate.

Pastry bag: A cone-shaped bag that can be used with fillings, whipped cream, and some doughs. Various-shaped tips are often placed in the small end of the cone in order to create a design for what is being piped out of the bag. Pastry bags can be made of numerous materials, including plastic and canvas lined with plastic.

Pith: The bitter white layer that is between the outer peel and the flesh of citrus fruits.

Poaching: A **cooking method** typically reserved for delicate foods done in liquid set to below the **boiling** point. By not allowing the liquid to **boil** and move rapidly, poaching is more gentle on the food.

Puff pastry: A very flaky dough made by rolling and folding layers of a yeast dough and fat, usually butter, a number of times. This creates hundreds of super thin layers of dough and fat. When cooked, the moisture in the butter releases steam and causes the layers to separate from each other and become crispy as they rise.

R

Ramekin: An individual baking dish in which food is cooked and served. The food may be either hot or cold and can be sweet or savory. Ramekins are typically ceramic and hold between two and six ounces.

Reduce: The process of allowing a liquid to **simmer** and **evaporate** some of its water in order to concentrate the flavors of the remaining liquid.

Render: To slowly heat animal fat to allow the fat to melt and separate from any solids. This flavorful fat is then used as an ingredient in cooking. As the fat liquefies, the remaining bits shrink and become crispy and flavorful. These bits, called cracklings, are also great as an ingredient or just as a snack.

Residual heat: Once an item is removed from a heat source, it will continue to cook due to the item being hotter than room temperature. This extra heat causes carry-over cooking. This is when an item such as a roast will continue to raise its internal temperature after being removed from the oven.

Rice vinegar: An Asian vinegar produced from fermenting rice. These vinegars are less acidic than most western vinegars. Seasoned rice vinegar has added salt and sugar, which makes it even milder.

Roasting: A **cooking method** where food is placed, uncovered, in an oven and allowed to cook. Roasted items typically are well browned on the outside. Vegetables or tender cuts of meat that do not benefit from a moist cooking method are often roasted.

Rough chop: A term used to describe the size and shape of a knife cut. Items that are rough chopped are similar in size but do not need to be uniform in shape. A rough chop is used in home-style dishes such as stews or in items that will be pureed later.

Roux: A thickener made from equal parts of fat and flour that has been cooked. For most applications, a roux is cooked over medium-low heat until nutty in smell. The fat is often butter or oil, but other fats can add more flavor. An example of this would be to use turkey fat to make your roux for turkey gravy. A general rule is that one pound of roux will thicken one gallon of liquid.

S

Salad shrimp: A general term used to describe tiny shrimp sold completely peeled and deveined.

Sauté: Meaning "to jump," a **cooking method** where food is cooked in a small amount of oil in a preheated pan. The food is kept in motion, either by flipping the pan or by stirring, so that all surfaces of the food come in contact with the heat. This method is good for quickly cooking tender meats and vegetables. Sautéing is usually done in a sauté pan.

Scalded, milk: Milk that has been heated to just below the **boiling** point. In the past, milk was often scalded to prevent souring, but now it's typically done to raise the temperature of the milk.

Sear: To quickly brown an item, usually meat, with very high heat. This can be done on a grill or broiler, in a pan, or in the oven. This browning develops flavor and color. Searing does not lock in juices, which is a common misconception.

Season: This is done to cast-iron pans to protect the pan and prevent sticking. Fat is added to the pan, and then the pan is heated. Through this process the pores of the metal open up and bond with the fat. Any excess fat is wiped out of the pan. Seasoning can also take place naturally as high-fat foods are cooked in a pan.

Semolina: A more coarse flour made from durum wheat. It's usually used in the making of high-quality pasta.

Shallot: A member of the onion family with a milder flavor than most onions. They grow similar to garlic with a number of **cloves** in one head but have layers like onions.

Shallow frying: A **cooking method** where food is cooked in hot oil. It's different from **deep-frying** in that the oil level is only about half the height of the food, and it's always done on a stovetop. In this method, the food comes in contact with the bottom of the pan, promoting further browning. Food cooked in this method also must be turned over to ensure even cooking because food above the oil will not cook.

Shock: The process of quickly cooling a **blanched** or cooked food to stop the cooking. Shocking is usually done under cold running water or in a bath of ice water. Food that has been shocked is often briefly reheated before being served.

Shred: This is the process of reducing the size of an object into relatively long, thin strips. It is often done to hard cheeses such as Parmesan and firm vegetables such as carrots. Either a box grater or a food processor is a good tool for this job.

Shrinkage: As meats cook, the proteins contract and force out moisture and cause a reduction in size. This is natural, but cooking a meat slowly at a low temperature can result in less shrinkage and loss of yield, than quick cooking at a higher temperature.

Simmering: A **cooking method** done at just below the **boiling** point of water. The liquid is at about 185 degrees, and small bubbles are just breaking the surface. This method is used for items too delicate for boiling, but not so fragile as to need to be **poached**. Simmering is also used to cook soups or reduce sauces.

Slurry: A mixture of **cornstarch** combined with an equal amount of cool liquid. This mixture is then stirred into a **simmering** liquid as a thickener. A slurry is used because adding straight cornstarch would result in clumping, as the cornstarch cooks as soon as it's heated.

Star tip: A metal or plastic piece that fits into the small end of a **pastry bag** to shape items being squeezed out into a multipointed star shape.

Statler: The breast of a bird with the first section of the wing (drumette) still attached.

Steaming: A **cooking method** in which food is placed on a rack or in a basket above **boiling** or **simmering** water in a closed container. This method helps foods maintain their shape, texture, and nutrients.

Steel: A tool used for **honing** the edge of a knife. A steel is a long, pointed rod along which the length of a knife's blade is run at an angle to straighten the edge. The rod is attached to a handle for easy gripping. Look for models with a large plastic guard to protect your hand while using the steel.

Stew: A combination **cooking method** very similar to **braising**. Done with smaller pieces of tough meat rather than one large piece. First the meat is **sautéed** to brown it and develop flavor and color. It is then finished by adding liquid and cooking slowly until the meat is tender. Beef stew is the most common dish made using this method.

Stir-fry: A **cooking method** used in Asian cuisine of cooking food over very high heat, often in a **wok**. The food to be stir-fried is usually tender and cut small so that it will cook quickly but still maintain crispness.

Stock: A flavorful liquid made from **simmering** meat or seafood scraps and bones with vegetables and **aromatics** such as bay leaves, thyme, peppercorns, and parsley stems. Stock is used as a base for soups and sauces.

Strainer: A perforated bowl or cone used for removing liquids from solids such as the water from cooked pasta. Fine strainers are used to remove unwanted solids from liquids such as soup, giving the food a smoother or finer consistency.

Sushi mat: A network of thin bamboo sticks held together with string to form an easily rolled mat. It is used to help form sushi, with **nori** or rice placed on it, filled, and then rolled. The mat is removed from the sushi before sealing and serving.

Sweat: To slowly cook vegetables over low heat in a small amount of oil, causing them to release their juices and cook without browning.

Sweet Soy Sauce: Available in Asian markets and larger supermarkets, this soy sauce has sweetness and additional richness from the addition of brown sugar or molasses.

T

Tahini: A paste made from ground sesame seeds. Tahini is used as a flavoring in Middle Eastern cooking.

Tang: The part of a knife blade that extends into the handle. High quality knives have a "full tang," where the metal of the blade extends through the entire handle, creating a longer lasting and more stable knife.

Temper: To equalize the temperature of two objects. This is often done with eggs by slowly adding small amounts of hot liquid into the eggs, while constantly stirring and raising their temperature. Once warm, this mixture may be stirred back into the hot liquid without as much concern that the eggs will scramble.

Texas toast: Presliced white bread that is thicker than normal sliced bread.

Translucent: Allowing light to pass through. Often referred to when cooking onions, which go from opaque to translucent as they are cooked.

W

Wasabi powder: Ground dried Japanese horseradish root. Green in color with a pungent, spicy taste.

Water bath: Used in **baking** to prevent items from cooking too quickly in a hot oven. The pan with the item to be **baked** is placed in another pan that has been partially filled with water. This water will never go above 212 degrees, which helps the product cook evenly. It's often used for baked goods thickened with eggs such as custards.

Western potatoes: Also known as baking, Idaho, or russet potatoes. They have a higher starch and moisture content than eastern potatoes and produce a flakier product. They are best for baked potatoes, French fries, and other dry **cooking methods**.

Wok: A round-bottomed pan used in Asian cooking. It can be used for **stir-frying, deep-frying, steaming**, or **braising**. A wok is typically used over a high flame, which engulfs the exterior surface of the pan and creates a surface that is evenly very hot. Food cooked in a wok is often stirred using long-handled utensils resembling spoons and shovels.

Wood Ear Mushroom: Usually available in dry chips at Asian markets, these mushrooms have a subtly crunchy texture and very little flavor. They tend to pick up flavors from items they are cooked with.

Z

Zest: The outer surface of a citrus fruit down to, but not including, the **pith**. Zests are high in flavor due to the presence of **aromatic** oils. They can be removed using a zester, peeler, or paring knife.

Things You Should Read

Books I Love

Better Homes and Gardens. *New Cook Book*. Des Moines: Meredith Books, 2006.
My first cookbook and the one I have used most for basic recipes.

Bourdain, Anthony. *Kitchen Confidential: Adventures in the Culinary Underbelly*. New York: Harper Perennial, 2001.
Some entertaining insights into the life and journey of one professional chef.

Boyle, Tish, and Timothy Moriarty. *Grand Finales: The Art of the Plated Dessert*. New York: Van Nostrand Reinhold, 1997.
Basically a coffee table book with photos of amazing desserts.

Brown, Alton. *I'm Just Here for the Food: Food + Heat = Cooking*. New York: Stewart, Tabori & Chang, 2002.
A great reference with recipes about the science of cooking.

Carroll, Ricki. *Home Cheese Making: Recipes for 75 Delicious Cheeses*. North Adams, MA: Storey Publishing, 2002.
You can actually make cheese in your kitchen. This informative and easy-to-understand book will show you how.

Child, Julia, Louisette Bertholle, and Simone Beck. *Mastering the Art of French Cooking*. New York: Alfred A. Knopf, 1964.
Julia Child's classic.

Dornenburg, Andrew, and Karen Page. *Becoming a Chef*. New York: Van Nostrand Reinhold, 1995.

Contains some sage advice and helpful information for anyone thinking of entering the restaurant industry.

Herbst, Sharon Tyler, and Ron Herbst. *Food Lovers Companion.* Hauppauge, New York: Barron's Educational Series, 2007.
　　Extensive food dictionary.

King Arthur Flour. *The King Arthur Flour Baker's Companion: The All-Purpose Baking Cookbook.* Woodstock, VT: Countryman Press, 2003.
　　A great baking reference for the home or professional cook.

McGee, Harold. *On Food and Cooking: The Science and Lore of the Kitchen.* New York: Fireside, 1984.
　　A great reference explaining the science behind food and cooking.

Rombauer, Irma S., Marion Rombauer Becker, and Ethan Becker. *Joy of Cooking: All About Canning and Preserving.* New York: Scribner, 2002.
　　Techniques, tips, and recipes for making and preserving your own jams, jellies, pickles, and vegetables at home.

Ruhlman, Michael, Brian Polcyn, and Thomas Keller. *Charcuterie: The Craft of Salting, Smoking, and Curing.* New York: W. W. Norton, 2005.
　　Everything you ever wanted to know about bacon, sausages, confit, and deli meats.

Schlosser, Eric. *Fast Food Nation: The Dark Side of the All-American Meal.* New York: Perennial, 2002.
　　An eye-opening examination of the past and present of the American fast-food industry.

Trotter, Charlie, and Tim Turner. *Charlie Trotter's Vegetables.* Berkeley, CA: Ten Speed Press, 1996.
　　Unbelievable close-up photographs of amazing food.

Periodicals to Check Out

CIA Pro Chef Smart Brief: electronic newsletter with the best food articles from around the country.

Cooks Illustrated: focuses on the science behind cooking.

Edible Communities: a group of regional magazines featuring local and sustainable agriculture and cooking.

Food Arts: free to culinary professionals; showcases the art of food.

Great Web Sites:

bbc.co.uk/food	BBC Food
CIAprochef.com	Culinary Institute of America professional site
epicurious.com	Great reference from *Gourmet* and *Bon Appétit* magazines
foodandwine.com	*Food and Wine* magazine
foodnetwork.com	The Food Network site

Index

CPSIA information can be obtained at www.ICGtesting.com
Printed in the USA
LVOW12s2104080914

403050LV00001B/136/P